Selected Letters

JOHN DONNE (1572–1631) developed one of the most distinctive and remarkable poetic voices of the English Renaissance. He also became a leading churchman: having been born and bred a Catholic (his mother was descended from Thomas More), he began asserting his loyalty to the Church of England in his twenties and was appointed Dean of St Paul's at the age of forty-nine. The first edition of his verse, which was published posthumously in 1633, contained a number of elegies commemorating him as one of the greatest preachers of his age. In his private life, however, he was dogged by insecurity and loss: in 1574 his mother's uncle was executed for saying Mass; ten years later one of her brothers narrowly avoided the same fate; and when Donne was twenty-one or so, his own brother died in Newgate, where he had been sent for harbouring a priest. Then, in 1601, Donne married the fifteen-year-old Ann More without her family's knowledge, precipitating a period of poverty and dependence which ended only with his ordination in 1615. Horrified by religious extremism, he occupied a moderate, central position in the fierce religious disputes of his day, enabling his parishioner Izaak Walton to present him, in the first edition of his *Life and Death of Dr Donne*, as a man entirely without party allegiances who devoted himself to preaching and acts of charity.

P.M. OLIVER is the author of *Donne's Religious Writing: A Discourse of Feigned Devotion* (Longman 1997).

Fyfield*Books* present poetry and prose by great as well as sometimes overlooked writers from British and Continental literatures. Clean texts at affordable prices, Fyfield*Books* make available authors whose works endure within our literary tradition.

The series takes its name from the Fyfield elm mentioned in Matthew Arnold's 'The Scholar Gypsy' and in his 'Thyrsis'. The elm stood close to the building in which the Fyfield series was first conceived in 1971.

> *Roam on! The light we sought is shining still.*
> *Dost thou ask proof? Our tree yet crowns the hill,*
> *Our Scholar travels yet the loved hill-side*

from 'Thyrsis'

Jᴏʜɴ Dᴏɴɴᴇ

Selected Letters

edited by P.M. Oliver

ROUTLEDGE
New York

Published in USA and Canada in 2002 by
Routledge
711 Third Avenue
New York, NY 10017
www.routledge-ny.com

Routledge is an imprint of the Taylor & Francis Group

By arrangement with Carcanet Press Ltd.

First published in Great Britain
in 2002 by
Carcanet Press Limited

This impression 2002

Text, introduction and editorial matter © P.M. Oliver 2002

The right of P.M. Oliver
to be identified as the editor of this
work has been asserted by him in accordance with
the Copyright, Designs and Patents Act of 1988

Cataloguing-in-Publication data is available from the Library of Congress.

ISBN 0-415-94227-6 (hb), 0-415-94228-4 (pb).

Printed and bound by SRP Limited, England

Contents

Introduction

JOHN DONNE (1572–1631) was the greatest English Renaissance writer of non-dramatic verse with the exception of John Milton and, perhaps, Edmund Spenser. There are more extant manuscripts of Donne's verse than of the work of any other poet of the period. Even contemporaries who were inclined to regard poetry as somewhat beneath them felt compelled to admire Donne's unique talents. In 1634 one enthusiast (George Garrard, the addressee of a number of the letters printed here) described poetry 'such as Dean Donne writ in his younger days' as 'very transcendent'.[1] Although Garrard did not choose to specify what he particularly admired about Donne, there is no reason to suppose that the features which modern readers have identified in his verse – its tightly knotted thought, arresting use of language, rich variety of personae and restless formal experimentation – were any less popular in his own time.

Garrard was correct in believing that Donne's verse, or most of it, was the product of his 'younger days'. In his forties Donne largely turned his back on versifying and reinvented himself as a clergyman, becoming one of the two most celebrated mainstream preachers of his time (the other was Lancelot Andrewes, who died in 1626). The sermons Donne delivered as Dean of St Paul's made him popular with fastidious courtiers and the London churchgoing public alike. In an attempt to voice the feeling of general loss occasioned by his death, a number of minor poets wrote tributes for inclusion in the first (posthumous) edition of his verse. These extravagantly flattering pieces were designed to articulate, among other things, the sense that to hear Donne deliver a sermon was to witness history in the making. One of them evokes the experience with a reference to the great preacher-saint of Christian antiquity: 'Golden Chrysostom was alive again.'[2] It's a compliment Donne would have relished. Chrysostom was one of his favourite Fathers of the Church, and he never tired of citing him in his sermons.

---

1 *The Earl of Strafforde's Letters and Dispatches*, edited by William Knowler, 2 vols (1739), I, p.338
2 *Poems by J.D. with elegies on the authors death* (1633), p.401

It would, however, have required prescience of no mean order to mark out such a path for Donne in the 1570s. He was born into an unequivocally Catholic family. On his mother's side he was descended from Thomas More, the former Chancellor of England executed for his allegiance to the old religion in 1536. (Donne admired his martyred ancestor enormously, calling him 'a man of the most tender and delicate conscience that the world saw since Augustine'.)[1] His great-uncle Thomas Heywood was executed for saying Mass only a couple of years after Donne was born, and both of his maternal uncles became Jesuits; one of them was hunted down and imprisoned in the Tower in 1584, avoiding execution, it has been suggested, solely as a result of having been page to the Princess Elizabeth years before.

Those who came into contact with the child Donne – evidently something of a prodigy – would probably have thought him more likely to preside over the Catholic mission to England than the fortunes of St Paul's Cathedral. They may even have predicted a martyr's death for him. (He would later describe how his 'first breeding and conversation' had been with 'men of a suppressed and afflicted religion, accustomed to the despite of death, and hungry of an imagined martyrdom'; he had, he said, been 'ever kept awake in a meditation of martyrdom'.)[2] At the age of about twelve Donne was sent, with his slightly younger brother Henry, to Hart Hall, Oxford and then, possibly via Cambridge, to Thavies Inn, one of the inns of chancery affiliated to Lincoln's Inn, to which he transferred in 1592. Like Hart Hall, the inns of court and chancery were known haunts of Catholics, and in 1593 Henry was caught sheltering a priest in his room at Thavies Inn and taken to Newgate, where he quickly died from the plague. The elder Donne still had Catholic tutors at this time according to Izaak Walton, his first biographer, and they 'were advised to instil into him particular principles of the Romish Church, of which those tutors professed (though secretly) themselves to be members'.[3] From the outset Donne knew the power of religious division – and his mother's refusal to abandon her Catholicism even when, long after he had abandoned his, she came to live with him at the deanery, ensured that he would never forget it.

Perhaps Donne's tutors were overzealous and inadvertently put him off Catholicism altogether. Perhaps it was experiences such as his brother's

1 *Biathanatos*, edited by Ernest W. Sullivan (1984), p.62
2 *John Donne: The Major Works*, edited by John Carey (2000), pp.149, 190
3 *Izaak Walton: Selected Writings*, edited by Jessica Martin (1997), p.41

death that did it. Whatever the cause, at some point in the 1590s he turned his back on the faith of his fathers and began the slow process of attaching himself to the Church of England. Exactly how long this took is now impossible to tell. It has been argued with some plausibility that he retained vestiges of Catholic belief well into the seventeenth century, but he was considered enough of a Protestant to be offered the post of secretary to the Lord Keeper, Sir Thomas Egerton, in 1597 or 1598: having played a prominent part in the prosecution of high-profile Catholics such as Mary, Queen of Scots and Edmund Campion, Egerton would not have wished to harbour a known recusant among his staff. In the event Donne filled the post of secretary very capably until he was sacked at the end of 1601 for marrying the fifteen-year-old Ann More without her family's knowledge.

It is no exaggeration to say that Donne did not recover from the effects of his clandestine marriage until he took orders in the Church of England in January 1615: the King was still holding his imprudent marriage against him in 1608 (see Letter XXVIII), and despite his cordial relations with a number of patrons, there was no discernible change in his fortunes over the next few years. The period of nearly a decade and a half between his marriage and his ordination was marked by persistent poverty and the humiliating necessity of reliance on the generosity of others, as many of his letters testify. By presenting himself as a candidate for ordination in the winter of 1614–15, Donne made sure that he and his longsuffering family would never again depend on charity to scrape a living. (His wife was prevented from seeing him at the height of his fame, dying when he was only two years into his ministry.) Moreover, by being appointed a royal chaplain soon after his ordination, Donne was guaranteed regular contact with the very circles in which he felt most at home.

It did not take him long to make his name. When James I decided, in September 1622, that an outdoor sermon at Paul's Cross was the best means of publicising new measures to curb inflammatory preaching, it was Donne who was chosen to defend the royal line. As it happens, we have the testimony of the letter-writer John Chamberlain to the effect that the sermon was a success. Chamberlain does mention, however, that Donne seemed oddly ill at ease when dealing with the new measures: 'he gave no great satisfaction, or – as some say – spake as if himself were not so well satisfied.' By then Donne had been Dean of St Paul's for almost a year, and was a supremely confident performer in the pulpit. Chamberlain had also witnessed his first appearance at Paul's Cross in March 1617, though even this had been 'exceedingly well liked generally'. (Chamberlain's praise is all the more conspicuous in the light of his censorious attitude to other preachers' performances.) Nor are the two Donne delivered at Paul's Cross the only sermons of his to have met with Chamberlain's approval. He pronounced Donne's first effort at the Cathedral in June 1622 'a very good sermon'; it was, he wrote, one of a number the new dean had preached 'with great concourse'. Of the homily Donne preached to mark the dedication of a new chapel at Lincoln's Inn, where he had been Divinity Reader at the time of his appointment to St Paul's, Chamberlain remarked: 'The Dean of Paul's made an excellent sermon (they say) concerning dedications.'[1] Within only a few years of his ordination, a sermon of Donne's was an event not to be missed.

*

Despite the fact that he enjoyed increasing celebrity from around 1617 until his death, most of Donne's letters would probably have been lost to posterity were it not for his son's desire to gain fame and make money from his unpublished writing. As it is, the two hundred or so letters which have come down to us (154 as a direct result of the younger John Donne's assiduity in editing two volumes of letters, one exclusively of his father's) represent one of the first two really significant collections of correspondence by an English literary figure. (The other – Sir Philip Sidney's – has nothing like the width of appeal of Donne's.)

As a collection Donne's letters are valuable for the glimpses that they offer us of his personality – a personality which is at least as much concealed as it is revealed by the poses struck in his verse. On the evidence of its defiant tone, for instance, Sir Edmund Gosse had no hesitation in assigning 'The Canonisation', one of Donne's most admired poems, to the period of his marriage,[2] but he overlooked the fact that Donne loved playing with poetic disguises more than most. (In fact we now know that 'The Canonisation' could have been written at almost any time between the late 1590s and 1614.)

Even in Donne's extant sermons the sense that a role is being acted out is so strong that inferences about the role-playing preacher himself can only be made with considerable tentativeness. Perhaps this overlap is not surprising given both the stylistic continuities between the poems and the

---

1 *The Letters of John Chamberlain*, edited by N.E. McClure, 2 vols (1939), II, pp.451, 67, 443, 500
2 Edmund Gosse, *The Life and Letters of John Donne*, 2 vols (1899), I, p.117

sermons and the propensity of the sermons for striking the kind of poses familiar to readers from the poems. Take one of Donne's more famous attempts to instil fear of divine judgement into his hearers:

> If there be a minute of sand left (there is not), if there be a minute of patience left, this minute that is left is that eternity which we speak of: upon this minute dependeth that eternity. And this minute, God is in this congregation and puts his ear to every one of your hearts, and hearkens what you will bid him say to yourselves – whether he shall bless you for your acceptation or curse you for your refusal of him this minute. For this minute makes up your century, your hundred years, your eternity, because it may be your last minute.[1]

The passage resembles moments in Donne's Holy Sonnets – 'What if this present were the world's last night?', for example – where there is an overt acknowledgement that a hypothesis is being used to stimulate a particular state of mind. The key difference is that in the sermon Donne is addressing his congregation very publicly while the speaker of the poem is supposedly addressing his soul in the privacy of internal dialogue.

There are passages of unmistakably personal import in the sermons, but even these are aspects of Donne's overarching rhetorical purposes: we can never be absolutely sure how to read them. Donne will have told his congregations only what he wished them to hear. And since our texts of almost all the sermons are based on versions Donne wrote up after delivering them, we can be equally certain that he provided readers with what he wished them to believe he had said, a factor which greatly increases the similarity between the sermons and the poems.

The extent to which Donne, in his sermons and poems, sought to produce particular effects on his hearers or readers is what more than anything else makes the self-exposure we encounter in the letters so riveting. Not that the letters lack a sense of audience: on one occasion when Donne seems momentarily to lose consciousness of his addressee, he has the good grace to notice his lapse and blames it on the fact that he has been working on a sermon and is still in homiletic mode (Letter LXXVI). The salient point is that when Donne unburdened himself to his confidants in his letters, he found artifice to be largely unnecessary. We only have to compare his manner of addressing his friends with the way in which he wrote to potential and actual patrons and benefactors to see how he

---

1 *The Sermons of John Donne*, ed. George R. Potter and Evelyn M. Simpson, 10 vols (1953–62), VII, pp.368–9

looked when not wearing a mask. In a letter to Goodyer dated 1608, he confesses that he is writing

> by the side of her whom, because I have transplanted into a wretched fortune, I must labour to disguise that from her by all such honest devices as giving her my company and discourse. Therefore I steal from her all the time which I give this letter and it is therefore that I take so short a list and gallop so fast over it.
>
> (Letter XXIV)

The objectivity with which he views what he has inflicted on Ann by marrying her is totally unexpected (especially if we come to this letter after making the acquaintance of the abrasively confident bridegroom presented in Letters V and VI), and momentarily unnerving.

Donne does not scruple to reprimand a close friend of his later years, Ann Cockayn, for presuming too much on the likelihood of his being able to advance the career of her sons' tutor, a Mr Hazard (Letter XCV). In his indignation he repeats a snippet of a conversation between him and Hazard in order to give Mrs Cockayn an idea of what Hazard is like when away from her:

> I told him that my often sicknesses had brought me to an inability of preaching, and that I was under a necessity of preaching twelve or four-teen solemn sermons every year to great auditories at Paul's and to the judges and at court, and that therefore I must think of conferring some-thing upon such a man as may supply my place in these solemnities: 'and surely,' said I, 'I will offer them no man in those cases which shall not be at least equal to myself, and, Mr Hazard, I do not know your faculties.' He gave me this answer: 'I will not make comparisons, but I do not doubt but I should give them satisfaction in that kind.'

Behind Donne's narration of the heated exchange is the pressure of his frustration and annoyance with Mrs Cockayn for mistaking him and being, as he sees it, deceived by Hazard. It causes him to descend to unchar-acteristic coarseness: in this matter, he says, his honour is 'as chaste and untouched as the best maidenhead in the world'. As if unaware of his own tone, Donne accuses Mrs Cockayn of venting her 'indignation and displea-sure' towards him.

The letter to Ann Cockayn has all the urgency and conviction of real communication and misunderstanding. By contrast, when Donne writes to the influential royal favourite James Hay to ask for his help in securing a vacant secretaryship, he adopts a stance of self-abasing devotion to Hay which now sounds highly artificial. 'This descent of your Lordship and your taking knowledge of so unuseful a servant as I am,' he assures Hay, 'gives me contentment and satisfaction enough and, so I may be sure to hold that room which your Lordship affords me in yourself, I care not to be anything else' (Letter XXVII). Even when he thanks Hay for his willingness to assist him and is forced to allude to the King's belief that his marriage remains an obstacle, Donne's desire for Hay's continued patronage makes him careful to maintain his sycophantic poise: 'I am, my Lord, somewhat more worthy of your favour than I was at first because every degree of your Lordship's favour is a great dignity' (Letter XXVIII). However, the stiffness and forced composure are still characteristics of the real Donne – a different, younger Donne who was compelled to beg for assistance with finding employment as opposed to an older, more powerful one to whom others could look for such assistance.

As these examples show, the figure cut by Donne in his letters is not always very edifying. Nor are his more questionable qualities on display only in his dealings with patrons. In an early letter in which he condoles with his most trusted confidant, Henry Goodyer, on the death of the latter's wife, he expresses his relief at having been so little acquainted with the dead woman since this will ensure that he has 'no more additions to sorrow'; he himself merits more comfort, he claims, than the bereaved husband (Letter XII). It has to be said that Donne does not emerge well from any of his epistolary attempts at consolation (with the possible exception of Letter LXXVIII). Writing to Mrs Cockayn on the death of one of her sons, he refers to how she had felt compelled, after being deserted by her husband, to hide their seven sons away in places such as Bath in case he came back for them: 'The perverseness of the father put you to such a necessity of hiding your sons as that this son is scarce more out of your sight by being laid underground than he was before' (Letter XC). Donne's determination to press home this maladroit thought leads him to attempt what looks suspiciously like a ponderous and ill-timed joke: 'and perchance you have been longer time, at some times, from meeting and seeing one another in this world than you shall be now from meeting in the glory of the Resurrection. That may come sooner than you looked he should come from the Bath.' The best that can be said is that Donne sounds as if he is at least making an effort to put himself in his friend's position. Tact, not selflessness, is what is missing.

Donne's self-involvement is not always of the repellent kind on display in the letter to the recently bereaved Goodyer. Writing to him a couple of years later, he describes his own circumstances in a way likely to elicit a measure of sympathy, if only because this is not his concern. His object at the outset is to review his recent achievements as dispassionately as possible:

> Every Tuesday I make account that I turn a great hour-glass and consider that a week's life is run out since I writ. But if I ask myself what I have done in the last watch, or would do in the next, I can say nothing. If I say that I have passed it without hurting any, so may the spider in my window.

(Letter XXV)

Donne's mood in this letter is also made darker, and perhaps more sympathetic still, by the guilty self-questioning stemming from one of his perennial concerns, the importance of being productively employed. By now self-analysis had become a deeply ingrained habit, and the results it produced were frequently far from encouraging for the analyst himself.

The letters are valuable, too, for the access they provide to Donne's thinking during various critical phases of his life. One, dating from January 1631, throws a disturbing light on his final appearance in the pulpit, an episode celebrated by Walton in his biography. At the height of his illness that winter, Donne still planned to fulfil his obligation of preaching at court on the first Friday of Lent, and, when the day came, mounted the pulpit against the wishes of friends, who tried to dissuade him on the grounds that delivering the sermon would hasten his death – which it probably did. What readers of Letter XCIII are enabled to appreciate is that this likely consequence of delivering the sermon in so frail a state was one which Donne had not merely foreseen but positively welcomed. His preaching ministry was everything to him: a common refrain of his sermons is, 'Woe is unto me if I preach not the gospel.' Coincidentally, this cry of St Paul's was the motto of the early Elizabethan bishop, John Jewel, who had also expressed the hope that preaching might be the death of him.[1] For Donne, as for Jewel, a pulpit death would have been the ultimate fulfilment of his mission.[2]

Without the letters we would not know that it was Donne's disgust with William Barlow's official defence of the oath of allegiance that impelled him to write *Pseudo-Martyr*, his own defence of the oath published in 1610 (Letter XXXI). It emerges during the course of the letter in ques-

---

1 *The Works of John Jewel*, edited by J. Ayre, 4 vols (1845–50), IV, p.xxi
2 Walton printed a shorter version of Letter XCIII in the first (1640) edition of his *Life of Donne*.

tion that he feels no great sympathy for the government line: the other side also has a good case. The letter reveals, in a way in which nothing Donne wrote for publication could afford to do, that while he was engaged in writing pro-government polemic aimed at Catholic readers, and even (in the case of his satirical fantasy *Ignatius His Conclave*) crudely anti-Catholic invective, he found himself in reality on the margins of the dispute, painfully torn between both parties to it. Indeed, in a letter written at about the same time as his critique of Barlow's scholarship, he tells Goodyer that the Catholic and Protestant Churches 'are sister teats of [God's] graces, yet both diseased and infected, but not alike', and proceeds to analyse and compare them, as Churches, in a disarmingly dispassionate manner (Letter XXX). That he was genuinely interested in the cause of interdenominational harmony at this time is evident from the postcript to Letter XXIX, in which he asks Goodyer to try to get him a copy of a book written by Georg Cassander, a member of the group of liberal Catholics based at Cologne in the middle years of the sixteenth century. It so happens that Donne mistakes the author, but his description of the book as having been written in connection with the Colloquy of Poissy, a brave attempt to reconcile French Catholics and Calvinists in which Cassander was involved, is sufficient proof of the active nature of his interest.

Although Donne was not entirely alone in having such interests, they were dangerously unorthodox in the first decade of the seventeenth century. When his friend Joseph Hall published *The Old Religion* in 1628, he inadvertently provoked a storm of controversy by referring to Rome as 'a true visible Church'.[1] On the whole Protestants still believed that the faith of Catholics prevented them from being saved; if they were saved at all, it was by default – by their ignorance of their errors. This is not the place to trace the reasons why Donne himself never doubted that Catholics could be saved, though it would be odd if his own rich Catholic patrimony and his mother's adherence to her Catholicism (and perhaps also his reverence for the memory of his father – see Letter LXV) were not contributory factors. What Donne's letters confirm is that, in his views as in his verse, he was anything but conventional.

Less momentous, but still of great interest for readers of the sermons, is the confirmation contained in a letter of autumn 1622 that those who had thought Donne lacking in enthusiasm for the King's *Directions to Preachers* had been absolutely right: writing a few weeks after the event, he expresses

---

1 *The Works of … Joseph Hall*, edited by Philip Wynter, 10 vols (1863), VIII, p.639

dissatisfaction with his performance in the September sermon but tells his addressee that in the 'Powder Plot' sermon he has just delivered at Paul's Cross, he 'was left more to [his] own liberty' (Letter XXIV). Although it would have been dangerous to say so openly in the letter, he must have felt deep misgivings about defending official measures designed to curb the activity which he regarded as being at the very centre of Christian piety. Moreover, one thrust of the new measures was to prevent pulpit criticism of the proposed match between Prince Charles and the Spanish Infanta, and we know from Letters LXXIV and LXXV what Donne thought of *that*.

*

Informative and insightful though Donne's letters undoubtedly are, readers may be struck by the eccentricity of the mentality which gave rise to them in the first place. It gives him pleasure, Donne assures Goodyer in October 1607, to see a letter he has written to him lying on his desk even though there is no immediate prospect of its being sent (Letter XXI). Letter-writing was an obsession with him, and he regarded a letter he had written with something like awe. Committed to the notion that it was quite unnecessary to use letters as vehicles for the communication of news, that to use them for that purpose was to run the risk of contaminating them,[1] he instead used them to communicate himself.

In an early letter he tells Henry Wotton, a friend from Oxford days, that what he has written does not merely carry 'an assurance of myself to you' but that 'unchangeable friendship [...] may now in these few and ill lines deliver me unto you' (Letter I). Writing to the Duke of Buckingham to thank him for his part in securing the deanery of St Paul's for him, Donne describes his letter as his 'image'; to tear the letter would be to tear 'this picture of mine' (Letter LXXI). His elevated conception of letters and the heightened self-consciousness he experienced when writing them explain why he was so anxious about letters reaching their destination – and so upset when one went astray: in the letter to Wotton he says that, but for his sorrow over the recent deaths of a number of his friends, he would be 'griev[ing] for the loss of a poor letter' he had sent Wotton in Ireland which had not reached him because of his unexpectedly early return home; it would have conveyed Donne's 'love and services' to him. Better for that letter if it had never been sent.

---

1 See John Carey's essay, 'John Donne's Newsless Letters' (details in Appendix B: Further Reading).

Sometimes Donne's thinking on the subject of letters has a religious, not to say sacramental tinge. He compares the experience of writing a letter and not knowing whether it will reach its addressee with that of not knowing when he will die: with regard to the latter, however, it is his intention at all times, he says, to 'provide for [his] soul's last convoy' (Letter XXI), a remark which, by implication, equates the writing of a letter with the reception of the eucharist as viaticum. Another early letter offers its addressee the perception that letters are 'friendship's sacraments'; as with the sacraments, one should be in a constant state of loving readiness to receive them.[1] Spiritual communion between writer and addressee occurs when a letter is received, according to a verse-letter to Sir Henry Wotton composed in 1597–8 beginning 'Sir, more than kisses, letters mingle souls;/For thus friends absent speak'. Ordinarily a great changer of his mind, Donne never changed his mind about this. We find him, some fifteen years later, describing letters as the means 'by which we deliver over our affections and assurances of friendship and the best faculties of our souls' (Letter IL). He does, however, change his mind about the precise nature of the spiritual state from which his letters emanate. He uses letters, he says, to 'vent' his 'meditations' (Letter XXIII).[2] But as if the meditative state is not intense enough to figure the mentality which generates his best letters, he claims, in October 1607, that letter-writing is 'a kind of ecstasy' – at least 'when it is with any seriousness' (Letter XXI).

Donne will presumably have known when he was writing with due seriousness of intention, but it may be productive to ask what constituted appropriately serious subject matter. He certainly saw himself as a suitable subject, if the detailed accounts of the state of his mental and physical health contained in many letters are any sort of guide. (Donne is surely being disingenuous when he tells Mrs Cockayn, at the start of Letter XCIV, that he would feel very uncomfortable telling her about his health if she had not ordered him to do so.) As we might have expected, philosophy also qualified, as did religion, although he was surprisingly ready to joke about it. In a Latin letter of 1611 he writes that some of his works 'are now about to undergo their last judgement': some will be sent to purgatory, others to hell; the rest 'will collapse and dissolve into utter annihilation, something with which God does not threaten even the wickedest sinners'.[3]

---

1 Evelyn M. Simpson, *A Study of the Prose Works of John Donne*, 2nd edition (1948), p.311
2 See also the comments in Letters XXII and XXIV.
3 *Poems by J.D.*, p.352; my translation.

Unfortunately for enthusiasts, however, Donne's poetry does not seem to have occupied much of his thinking when he set about composing letters. Readers who trawl through those printed here in search of unambiguous references to his *Songs and Sonnets*, the poems which have attracted the most attention in recent times, are destined to feel especially cheated.

Scholars have proposed various explanations as to why Donne's poems get such scanty treatment in his letters. It has been argued that, in an age when the writing of verse was frequently regarded with hostility, Donne did not wish to be known as a poet and therefore suppressed all but the occasional mention of this particular use of his leisure. This suspicion is corroborated by his marked reluctance to follow a suggestion of Goodyer's that he should express his admiration of the Countess of Huntingdon in verse: 'that knowledge which she hath of me was in the beginning of a graver course than of a poet, into which (that I may also keep my dignity) I would not seem to relapse' (Letter XXX). The same thrust can be seen behind passages in two letters sent from Paris in April 1612 in which he discusses the storm created by the publication of his *Anniversaries*: he bitterly regrets the lapse of judgement which caused him to 'descend' to printing these fulsome pieces written to commemorate the daughter of his patron Sir Robert Drury (Letters XLIII and XLIV). When, a couple of years later, he is preparing to take orders and trying, in a move which has baffled many, to gather in all of his verse with a view to publication, he is keen that Lady Bedford should not hear of his intentions until it is too late for her to put a stop to the project (Letter LIX).

Conversely, in 1607 he had told his friend Magdalen Herbert that he was sending her a sonnet to accompany some 'holy hymns and sonnets', probably his *La Corona* sequence (Letter XX) – and the letter expressing his nervousness about not wanting to be known as a poet by the Countess of Huntingdon had contained verses written for Lady Bedford (admittedly he is still anxious that they should not cause him to be 'esteemed light' by those whose friendship he values). Versifying was not therefore off-limits as far as Donne's female patrons, or some of them, were concerned, even if it was a topic that called for delicate handling. And it remains hard to explain why he says so little about poetry in his letters to his close male friends. After all, he and Goodyer wrote a verse letter together; they exchanged prose Paradoxes and Problems (Letters III, XI and XIX); from time to time Donne sent him a 'rag of verses' (Letter XIX); we know Donne sent someone, probably Henry Wotton, copies of his Paradoxes, Elegies and Satires (Letter III). Given that his friends were so well acquainted with this side of Donne, why the silence?

The answer I favour is not, perhaps, a very consoling one. Despite the easily imaginable excitement which would be created today by the discovery of a hitherto unknown lyric of the calibre of 'The Anniversary' or 'The Sun Rising', Donne's letters impel us, I believe, to concede that even those of his poems which we value hugely had nothing like the importance for him which they have for us. We can be fairly confident that if the writing of verse had imparted a strong sense of the meaningfulness of his life during the Mitcham years,[1] he would have said so in his weekly letters to Goodyer. Although only a comparatively small number of these letters have survived, there is no reason to suppose that those which have gone astray would have told a markedly different story. As it is, the most Donne will say in the extant letters from this period is that writing 'A Litany' has proved an interesting distraction during his enforced 'imprisonment' in bed due to illness (Letter XXVI).

Of course, our hunger for insights into the process of composition can lead us to exaggerate the extent of Donne's reticence on the subject of his poetry. As we have seen, several of his letters had poems enclosed with them. Some letters positively illuminate specific poems. In the one describing the genesis of 'A Litany', he claims to have been motivated by the desire to steer a middle course between orthodox Protestant and Catholic viewpoints (another sign of his ecumenical interests), which would explain why parts of the poem so spectacularly fail to perform the balancing act required of it.

The quality of the poem he sends Goodyer for passing on to Lady Bedford breeds as much anxiety as the question of whether he can afford to write to Lady Huntingdon: 'if these verses be too bad, or too good, over or under her understanding and not fit, I pray, receive them as a companion and supplement of this letter to you.' In the two letters in which he responds to criticism of his *Anniversaries*, he stresses that his praise for Elizabeth Drury should not be taken too seriously for he had not even met her. Most tellingly of all, perhaps, he says in a brief letter sent to Sir Robert Ker in March 1625 that he has not at all enjoyed writing a hymn to mark the recent death of a leading courtier because he has not been able to give his poetic imagination free reign: 'You know my uttermost when it was best, and even then I did best when I had least truth for my subjects. In this present case there is so much truth as it defeats all poetry' (Letter LXXX). Put alongside Donne's comments about not having known

---

1 See headnote to Letter XIII.

Elizabeth Drury, the note to Ker constitutes a remarkable creative manifesto: poetry as baseless fantasy – the ultimate rebuttal of the 'autobiographical fallacy'. It also, once again, brings us close to the real Donne, with his implied rebuke to Ker for commissioning the poem and petulant suggestion that they should 'smother' it if it doesn't pass muster.

In that Donne's letters, or those which have survived, fail to provide the kind of information about works such as the *Songs and Sonnets* that modern readers would value, they are obviously not analogous to the letters of John Keats or Wilfred Owen, who routinely shared with their correspondents their feelings about what they were, or had been, writing. From another point of view, however, Donne's letters are at least the equal of Keats's and Owen's, for they give us an abundant sense of the personality and personal context from which his poems issued.

At times this amounts to striking verbal and thematic resemblances – such as those which connect the remark about letter-writing being 'a kind of ecstasy' and 'The Ecstasy', one of the best-known of the *Songs and Sonnets*. In the prose passage Donne goes on to define the experience of writing a letter as 'a departure and secession and suspension of the soul, which doth then communicate itself to two bodies', while the speaker of the poem describes how his own and his lover's souls had 'gone out' from their bodies in order to hang in the space between them and mingle, and ends by urging the two souls to return to the bodies they had temporarily abandoned. The time-scheme of 'The Ecstasy' is typically problematic, but both texts envisage the same basic process.

It would be fascinating to know whether Donne had recently composed 'The Ecstasy' when he sat down to write the letter. Perhaps the letter inspired the poem. Perhaps they were composed years apart. The perception of critical importance prompted by reading Donne's letters alongside his poems is that the language and ideas of the poems were not quite such bizarre developments as they can easily be made to appear. We know that Donne realised that his verse was unconventional (writing of his poems in Letter LIX, he calls himself 'startling'), but the letters dispel any idea that in his poetry he strained after an originality which did not come naturally to him. The originality lay in the man. It's a point about style and thought, not experience: to claim that 'The Ecstasy' and one of Donne's letters show linguistic and thematic similarities is not to endorse an autobiographical reading of the poem; rather, it highlights the way in which Donne's poems and letters are the products of different, related parts of the same creative mind.

So outmoded a critical approach is entirely justified: the notion of 'the death of the author', confidently announced towards the end of the twentieth century, was not lent much assistance by the canon of Donne's writing. Far from exemplifying the claim that 'writing is the destruction of every voice',[1] Donne's poetry and prose make us continuously aware of their author's distinctive tones. We are constantly encouraged to make connections between texts written in his own person and those in which he employs more or less elaborately fabricated modes of address. History has not dealt kindly with John Donne the younger, but he undoubtedly performed an invaluable service to readers when he bequeathed them 154 of his father's letters, thus putting them in a position to make some intriguing and pertinent connections.

---

1 Roland Barthes, *Image-Music-Text*, essays selected and translated by Stephen Heath (1977), p.142. (The quotation is from Barthes's seminal essay, 'The Death of the Author'.)

A Note on the Text

ALL OF THE LETTERS printed here have been transcribed from seventeenth-century printed texts or from old-spelling transcriptions. All spellings, including those of place names, have been modernised. In the interests of consistency, however, no attempt had been made to replace archaic words with their modern equivalents: although it would have been possible, for example, to replace 'accompt' (p.8) with 'account', it would hardly have been legitimate to render 'evangiles' (p.17) as 'gospels'.

Punctuation has been silently emended: the seventeenth-century texts of Donne's letters look forbiddingly over-punctuated to modern eyes, and I have simplified or removed anything that I felt was likely to impede fluent reading. At times the result has been a deeply unhappy compromise. The punctuation of English Renaissance prose could afford to be flexible because its syntax was much looser than its modern counterpart: latinate rigidity had not yet set in.

The original texts of Donne's letters are for the most part printed unparagraphed, and paragraphing has therefore been supplied. I have silently corrected any obvious misprints and, on a small number of occasions, supplied missing words. However, where it is clear that more than a single word is missing, there has been no attempt to make good the omission. Initial letters and contracted forms of the first names of Donne's contemporaries ('Rob.', etc) have been expanded, except in the two instances (Sir G. Greseley; Mr W. Stanhope) where it has proved impossible to establish what the initial letter stood for.

For details of Donne's addressees and of individuals mentioned in the letters who were personally known to him, see Appendix A: Glossary of Names.

The Chronology of Donne's Letters

DONNE'S LETTERS are notoriously difficult to date, partly because in printing *Letters to Severall Persons of Honour* his son was not concerned with providing a chronological sequence; moreover, he readdressed a large number of letters and withheld the dates of some. (It is, of course, possible that he did not know them.) He also generally declined to provide dates for the letters printed in *A Collection of Letters made by Sir Tobie Mathews, Kt*, published nine years later.

Fortunately a number of twentieth-century academics, notably Professors Bald, Bennett and Shapiro (see Appendix B: Further Reading), did much to establish the likely chronology of the letters. However, uncertainties still abound, and the letters printed here are arranged in order of composition as far as it has been possible to ascertain this. Where only its probable year of composition is known, a letter will be found at the end of the chronological run for that year, after the more precisely dated or datable letters, except when this would make nonsense of what is written in them, where a chronological sequence has been attempted (Letter LIII clearly predates LIV, for example).

Selected Letters

Letter I. *To Sir Henry Wotton*   Autumn 1599

*The background to this, one of the few sixteenth-century letters attributed to Donne
which is certainly from his pen, is the Earl of Essex's abrupt return from Ireland in
September 1599 in defiance of the Queen's wishes. As a result of this dangerous
move on the part of the Earl, Wotton – one of his secretaries in Ireland – had arrived
back in England earlier than expected.*

Sir,
But that I have much earnest sorrow for the loss of many dear friends
in Ireland,[1] I could make shift to grieve for the loss of a poor letter of mine
which sought you there after your return, in which, though there were
nothing to be commended but that it was well suited for the place and
barbarous enough to go thither, yet it should have brought the thanks and
betrothed to you the love and services of one who had rather be honest
than fortunate. This letter hath a greater burthen and charge, for it carries
not only an assurance of myself to you but it begs a pardon that I have not
in these weeks sought you out in England by letters and acknowledged
how deep root the kindness of your letter hath taken in me. But as in
former innocent times estates of lands passed safely in few words (for these
many entangling clauses are either intended at least to prevent or breed
deceit), so unchangeable friendship, being ever the same and therefore not
subject to the corruption of these times, may now in these few and ill lines
deliver me unto you and assure you none hath better title than you in
                                    Your poor friend and lover.

Letter II. *Addressee unknown (Sir Henry Wotton?)*   1600

*This letter takes a contemptuous view of the court which would no doubt have
surprised Donne's employer, the Lord Keeper, but which harmonises with the
attitude of his Satires (written probably in the late 1590s). Moreover, the status he
claims to have vis-à-vis the court – that of visitor – is similar to the pose struck in*

---

1 These included Thomas Egerton, the son of Donne's employer, the Lord
Keeper, whose sword Donne bore at his funeral. They had both served on the
'Islands' Expedition in 1597.

the Satires. *At the same time, the letter resembles the poems in betraying a fascination with court life which warns us not to take Donne's disapproval at face value.*

Sir,

That love which went with you follows and overtakes and meets you. If words sealed up in letters be like words spoken in those frosty places where they are not heard till the next thaw, they have yet this advantage, that where they are heard, they are heard only by one or such as in his judgement they are fit for. I am no courtier for, without having lived there desirously, I cannot have sinned enough to have deserved that reprobate name. I may sometimes come thither and be no courtier as well as they may sometimes go to chapel and yet are no Christians. I am there now where, because I must do some evil, I envy your being in the country – not that it is a vice will make any great show here for they live at a far greater rate and expense of wickedness, but because I will not be utterly out of fashion and unsociable. I glean such vices as the greater men (whose barns are full) scatter, yet I learn that the learnedest in vice suffer some misery, for when they have reaped flattery or any other fault long, there comes some other new vice in request wherein they are unpractised. Only the women are free from this charge for they are sure they cannot be worse nor more thrown down than they have been. They have perchance heard that God will hasten his judgement for the righteous' sake, and they affect [like] not that haste, and therefore seek to lengthen out the world by their wickedness.

The court is not great, but full of jollity and revels and plays, and as merry as if it were not sick. Her Majesty is well disposed and very gracious in public to my Lord Mountjoy. My Lord of Essex and his train are no more missed here than the angels which were cast down from heaven, nor (for anything I see) likelier to return.[1] He withers still in his sickness and plods on to his end in the same pace where you left us. The worst accidents of his sickness are that he conspires with it, and that it is not here believed. That which was said of Cato, that his age understood him not, I fear may be averted [reversed] of your Lord,[2] that he understood not his

---

1 Following Essex's disgrace and banishment from court in 1599, he was for a time a prisoner of the Lord Keeper's at York House, where Donne himself lived and worked. ('Here' clearly means at court rather than at York House.)
2 See headnote to Letter I. Donne's own attitude to the Earl had evidently changed since the days of his military service under him (1596–7).

age, for it is a natural weakness of innocency that such men want [lack] locks for themselves and keys for others.

Letter III. *Addressee unknown (Sir Henry Wotton?)*   About 1600

With its allusions – rare in his extant correspondence – to what Donne has been writing, this letter paints a vivid picture of the way in which amateur writers exchanged their latest efforts. The shame Donne claims to feel on account of his Paradoxes[1] and amatory Elegies reflects his growing sensitivity to the stigma attached to such writing in respectable circles; his attitude to his satirical verse may be due to the fact that the printing of satires was proscribed in 1599.

Sir,

Only in obedience I send you some of my Paradoxes. I love you and myself and them too well to send them willingly, for they carry with them a confession of their lightness and your trouble and my shame. But indeed they were made rather to deceive time than her daughter truth, although they have been written in an age when anything is strong enough to over-throw her. If they make you to find better reasons against them, they do their office, for they are but swaggerers, quiet enough if you resist them. If perchance they be prettily gilt, that is their best, for they are not hatched.[2] They are rather alarums [warnings] to truth to arm her than enemies, and they have only this advantage to scape from being called ill things, that they are nothings. Therefore, take heed of allowing any of them lest you make another. Yet, sir, though I know their low price, except I receive by your next letter an assurance upon the religion of your friendship that no copy shall be taken for any respect of these or any other my composi-tions sent to you, I shall sin against my conscience if I send you any more. I speak that in plainness which becomes (methinks) our honesties and, therefore, call not this a distrustful but a free spirit. I mean to acquaint you with all mine, and to my Satires there belongs some fear, and to some Elegies, and these, perhaps, shame, against both which affections, although I be tough enough, yet I have a riddling disposition to be ashamed of fear

---

1 Lighthearted prose pieces with titles such as 'That Nature is our worst guide'.
2 Pun: (1) striped with gold and (2) born.

and afraid of shame. Therefore I am desirous to hide them without any over-reckoning of them or their maker. But they are not worth thus much words in their dispraise.

I will step to a better subject, your last letter, to which, I need not tell, I made no answer, but I had need excuse it. All your letter I embrace, and believe it when it speaks of yourself and when of me too, if the good words which you speak of me be meant of my intentions to goodness. For else, alas, no man is more beggarly in actual virtue than I. I am sorry you should (with any great earnestness) desire anything of P. Aretinus – not that he could infect, but that it seems you are already infected with the common opinion of him.[3] Believe me, he is much less than his fame and was too well paid by the Roman Church in that coin which he coveted most, where his books were by the Council of Trent forbidden, which, if they had been permitted to have been worn by all, long ere this had been worn out. His divinity was but a syrup to enwrap his profane books to get them passage. Yet in these books which have divine titles there is least harm, as in his letters most good. His others have no other singularity in them but that they are forbidden. The Psalms which you ask, if I cannot shortly procure you one to possess, I can and will at any time borrow for you.[4] In the meantime, sir, have the honour of forgiving two faults together: my not writing last time and my abrupt ending now.

Letter IV. *Addressee unknown (Sir Henry Wotton?)*   About 1600

Donne's proud boast of his literary independence at the start of this letter and his claim that he reads to 'enjoy idleness' need to be treated with some caution in the light of the number of learned borrowings in his writings. (His complaint that Dante consigned Pope Celestine V to purgatory merely for giving up the papacy may perhaps make more sense when read against the background of his criticism of court life in Letter II.)

---

3 Pietro Aretino's writings were a byword for obscenity.
4 Perhaps the version of the Psalms by Sir Philip Sidney and his sister, the Countess of Pembroke: Donne later wrote a poem expressing his admiration of their translation.

Sir,

I am no great voyager in other men's works, no swallower nor devourer of volumes nor pursuant of authors. Perchance it is because I find born in myself knowledge or apprehension enough for (without forfeiture or impeachment of modesty) I think I am bound to God thankfully to acknowledge it, to consider him and myself – as, when I have at home a convenient garden, I covet not to walk in others' broad meadows or woods, especially because it falls not within that short reach which my foresight embraceth to see how I should employ that which I already know. To travail [exert myself] for inquiry of more were to labour to get a stomach [appetite] and then find no meat at home.

To know how to live by the book is a pedantry, and to do it is a bondage, for both hearers and players are more delighted with voluntary than with set music, and he that will live by precept shall be long without the habit of honesty, as he that would every day gather one or two feathers might become brawn with hard lying before he make a feather bed of his gettings. That Earl of Arundel that last died (that tennis ball whom Fortune, after tossing and banding [striking to and fro], brickwalled into the hazard [caused to rebound into the opening]) in his imprisonment used more than much reading, and to him that asked him why he did so, he answered, he read so much lest he should remember something. I am as far from following his counsel as he was from Petruccio's,[1] but I find it true that after long reading I can only tell you how many leaves I have read. I do therefore more willingly blow and keep awake that small coal which God hath pleased to kindle in me than far off to gather a faggot of green sticks which consume without flame or heat in a black smother. Yet I read something, but indeed, not so much to avoid as to enjoy idleness.

Even when I begun to write these, I flung away Dante the Italian, a man pert [clever] enough to be beloved and too much to be believed. It angered me that Celestine, a pope so far from the manners of other popes that he left even their seat, should by the court of Dante's wit be attached [arrested] and by him thrown into his purgatory, and it angered me as much that in the life of a pope he should spy no greater fault than that, in the affectation [desire] of a cowardly security, he slipped from the great burthen laid upon him. Alas, what would Dante have him do? Thus we find the story related: he that thought himself next in succession by a trunk through

---

1 Possibly a reference to Shakespeare's *Taming of the Shrew*, it was well known that Arundel, a recusant who died in the Tower in 1595, had been dominated by his wife.

a wall whispered in Celestine's ear counsel to remove the papacy. Why should not Dante be content to think that Celestine took this for as immediate a salutation and discourse of the Holy Ghost as Abraham did the commandment of killing his son? If he will needs punish retiredness thus, what hell can his wit devise for ambition? And if white integrity merit this, what shall *male* [wrongly done] or *malum* [evil],[2] which Seneca condemns most, deserve? But as the Chancellor Hatton, being told after a decree made that his predecessor's was of another opinion, he answered, 'He had his genius and I had mine,' so say I of authors that they think and I think both reasonably, yet possibly both erroneously. That is manly, for I am so far from persuading, yea counselling, you to believe others that I care not that you believe not me when I say that others are not to be believed. Only believe that I love you and I have enough.

I have studied philosophy. Therefore, marvel not if I make such accompt [account] of arguments *quae trahuntur ab effectibus* [which are drawn from effects].

Letter V. *To Sir George More*   2 February 1602

In December 1601 Donne took the disastrous step of marrying Sir George More's sixteen-year-old daughter Ann without her family's knowledge. After the secret ceremony the bride returned to Loseley Park, the Mores' Surrey home, and in due course Donne chose the Earl of Northumberland, a close friend, to act as go-between and acquaint Sir George with the marriage. (By this time Donne himself was ill.) Bearing this far from tactful letter, Northumberland presented himself at Loseley early in February 1602.

Sir,

If a very respective fear of your displeasure and a doubt that my Lord[1] (whom I know, out of your worthiness, to love you much) would be so compassionate with you as to add his anger to yours did not so much increase my sickness as that I cannot stir, I had taken the boldness to have done the office of this letter by waiting upon you myself to have given

---

2 This passage may be defective, but the sense is clear.

---

1 The Lord Keeper, Sir Thomas Egerton.

you truth and clearness of this matter between your daughter and me, and to show to you plainly the limits of our fault, by which I know your wisdom will proportion the punishment.

So long since as her being at York House[2] this had foundation, and so much then of promise and contract built upon it as, without violence to conscience, might not be shaken. At her lying in town this last Parliament I found means to see her twice or thrice. We both knew the obligations that lay upon us, and we adventured equally, and about three weeks before Christmas we married. And as at the doing there were not used above five persons, of which, I protest to you by my salvation, there was not one that had any dependence or relation to you, so in all the passage of it did I forbear to use any such person who, by furthering of it, might violate any trust or duty towards you.

The reasons why I did not fore-acquaint you with it (to deal with the same plainness that I have used) were these: I knew my present estate less than fit for her; I knew, yet I knew not why, that I stood not right in your opinion; I knew that to have given any intimation of it had been to impossibilitate the whole matter; and then, having these honest purposes in our hearts and those fetters in our consciences, methinks we should be pardoned if our fault be but this, that we did not, by fore-revealing of it, consent to our hindrance and torment.

Sir, I acknowledge my fault to be so great as I dare scarce offer any other prayer to you in mine own behalf than this, to believe this truth, that I neither had dishonest end nor means. But for her whom I tender much more than my fortunes or life (else I would I might neither joy in this life nor enjoy the next), I humbly beg of you that she may not, to her danger, feel the terror of your sudden anger.

I know this letter shall find you full of passion, but I know no passion can alter your reason and wisdom, to which I adventure to commend these particulars: that it is irremediably done; that if you incense my Lord, you destroy her and me; that it is easy to give us happiness; and that my endeavours and industry, if it please you to prosper them, may soon make me somewhat worthier of her.

If any take the advantage of your displeasure against me and fill you with ill thoughts of me, my comfort is that you know that faith and thanks are due to them only that speak when their informations might do good, which now it cannot work towards any party. For my excuse I can say

---

2 Egerton's London house.

nothing except I knew what were said to you.

Sir, I have truly told you this matter, and I humbly beseech you so to deal in it as the persuasions of nature, reason, wisdom and Christianity shall inform you, and to accept the vows of one whom you may now raise or scatter – which are, that as my love is directed unchangeably upon her, so all my labours shall concur to her contentment, and to show my humble obedience to yourself.

Yours in all duty and humbleness,
J. Donne
From my lodging by the Savoy

Letter VI. *To Sir George More*   11 February 1602

Neither Donne's letter nor Northumberland's efforts at conciliation (see Letter V) were enough to persuade Sir George More to view his daughter's marriage in a favourable light; instead he prevailed upon Egerton to dismiss Donne from his service, started proceedings before the High Commission to test the legality of the marriage and had Donne thrown into the Fleet Prison, from where he sent this second letter.

Sir,

The inward accusations in my conscience that I have offended you beyond any ability of redeeming it by me and the feeling of my Lord's[1] heavy displeasure following it forceth me to write, though I know my fault make my letters very ungracious to you.

Almighty God, whom I call to witness that all my grief is that I have in this manner offended you and him, direct you to believe that which, out of an humble and afflicted heart, I now write to you. And since we have no means to move God, when he will not hear our prayers, to hear them but by praying, I humbly beseech you to allow by his gracious example my penitence so good entertainment as it may have a belief and a pity.

Of nothing in this one fault that I hear said to me can I disculp [exonerate] myself but of the contemptuous and despiteful purpose towards you which I hear is surmised against me. But for my dutiful regard to my late

---

1 Egerton's.

Lady,[2] for my religion and for my life I refer myself to them that may have observed them. I humbly beseech you to take off these weights and to put my fault into the balance alone, as it was done without the addition of these ill reports, and though then it will be too heavy for me, yet then it will less grieve you to pardon it.

How little and how short the comfort and pleasure of destroying is, I know your wisdom and religion informs you. And though perchance you intend not utter destruction, yet the way through which I fall towards it is so headlong that, being thus pushed, I shall soon be at bottom, for it pleaseth God, from whom I acknowledge the punishment to be just, to accompany my other ills with so much sickness as I have no refuge but that of mercy, which I beg of him, my Lord and you, which I hope you will not repent to have afforded me since all my endeavours and the whole course of my life shall be bent to make myself worthy of your favour and her love whose peace of conscience and quiet I know must be much wounded and violenced if your displeasure sever us.

I can present nothing to your thoughts which you knew not before but my submission, my repentance and my hearty desire to do anything satisfactory to your just displeasure, of which I beseech you to make a charitable use and construction.

Yours in all faithful duty and obedience,

J. Donne

From the Fleet

Letter VII. *To Sir Thomas Egerton*   12 February 1602

Sir George More's response to Donne's second letter was to cut off all contact with him. The next day Donne decided to sound out his employer using a more abject style than he had employed in his two letters to More. This is the first appearance in Donne's correspondence of a motif which was destined to make almost routine appearances in letters to potential patrons – that of a desire to be aided solely by the person to whom he is writing at the time.

---

2 Egerton's second wife, whom he married in October 1597 and who died in January 1600; she was Ann More's aunt.

Sir,

To excuse my offence, or so much to resist the just punishment for it as to move your Lordship to withdraw it, I thought till now were to aggravate my fault. But since it hath pleased God to join with you in punishing thereof with increasing my sickness, and that he gives me now audience by prayer, it emboldeneth me also to address my humble request to your Lordship that you would admit into your favourable consideration how far my intentions were from doing dishonour to your Lordship's house, and how unable I am to escape utter and present destruction if your Lordship judge only the effect and deed.

My services never had so much worth in them as to deserve the favours wherewith they were paid, but they had always so much honesty as that only this hath stained them. Your justice hath been merciful in making me know my offence, and it hath much profited me that I am dejected. Since then I am so entirely yours that even your disfavours have wrought good upon me. I humbly beseech you that all my good may proceed from your Lordship, and that since Sir George More, whom I leave no humble way unsought to regain, refers all to your Lordship, you would be pleased to lessen that correction which your just wisdom hath destined for me, and so to pity my sickness and other misery as shall best agree with your honourable disposition.

Almighty God accompany all your Lordship's purposes and bless you and yours with many good days.

Your Lordship's most dejected and poor servant,

J. Donne

From the Fleet

Letter VIII. *To Sir George More*   13 February 1602

The Lord Keeper had Donne released from prison, possibly because of the extent to which his health was suffering. Donne then wrote this rather presumptuous letter to More with a view to defending himself against malicious gossip. (Though written only the day after the previous letter, this, too, assures its recipient of Donne's wish to be dependent on him alone.)

Sir,

From you, to whom next to God I shall owe my health by enjoying, by your mediation, this mild change of imprisonment, I desire to derive all my good fortune and content in this world, and therefore, with my most unfeigned thanks, present to you my humble petition that you would be pleased to hope that, as that fault which was laid to me of having deceived some gentlewomen before and that of loving a corrupt religion are vanished and smoked away (as I assure myself, out of their weakness they are), and that as the Devil in the article of our death takes the advantage of our weakness and fear to aggravate our sins to our conscience, so some uncharitable malice hath presented my debts double at least.

How many of the imputations laid upon me would fall off if I might shake and purge myself in your presence! But if that were done, of this offence committed to you I cannot acquit myself, of which yet I hope that God (to whom for that I heartily direct many prayers) will inform you to make that use, that as of evil manners good laws grow, so out of disobedience and boldness you will take occasion to show mercy and tenderness. And when it shall please God to soften your heart so much towards us as to pardon us, I beseech you also to undertake that charitable office of being my mediator to my Lord,[1] whom, as upon your just complaint you found full of justice, I doubt not but you shall also find full of mercy, for so is the almighty pattern of justice and mercy equally full of both.

My conscience and such affection as in my conscience becomes an honest man emboldeneth me to make one request more, which is that by some kind and comfortable message you would be pleased to give some ease of the afflictions which I know your daughter in her mind suffers, and that (if it be not against your other purposes) I may with your leave write to her, for without your leave I will never attempt anything concerning her. God so have mercy upon me as I am unchangeably resolved to bend all my courses to make me fit for her, which, if God and my Lord and you be pleased to strengthen, I hope neither my debts, which I can easily order, nor anything else shall interrupt. Almighty God keep you in his favour and restore me to his and yours.

From my chamber, whither by your favour I am come,

J. Donne

---

1 Egerton.

Letter IX. *To Sir Thomas Egerton*   1 March 1602

Once he knew that the High Commission had decided in favour of the legality of his marriage, Donne wrote to Egerton again, and the interest of this 'elegant and pathetic letter' (as the Loseley Manuscript styles it) lies in its desperate attempt to incline Egerton to mercy by offering him an account of its writer's life which stresses his integrity. We can only speculate about the success of Donne's final paragraph, with its claim to know his addressee intimately: it was a ploy which had already failed to influence Sir George More.

Sir,
    That offence which was to God in this matter his mercy hath assured my conscience is pardoned. The Commissioners who minister his anger and mercy incline also to remit it.[1]
    Sir George More, of whose learning and wisdom I have good knowledge (and therefore good hope of his moderation), hath said before his last going that he was so far from being any cause or mover of my punishment or disgrace that, if it fitted his reputation, he would be a suitor to your Lordship for my restoring. All these irons are knocked off, yet I perish in as heavy fetters as ever whilst I languish under your Lordship's anger.
    How soon my history is dispatched! I was carefully and honestly bred; enjoyed an indifferent fortune; I had (and I had understanding enough to value it) the sweetness and security of a freedom and independency, without marking out to my hopes any place of profit; I had a desire to be your Lordship's servant by the favour which your good son's love to me obtained;[2] I was four years your Lordship's secretary, not dishonest nor greedy; the sickness of which I died is that I begun in your Lordship's house this love; where I shall be buried I know not. It is late now for me (but yet necessity, as it hath continually an autumn and a withering, so it hath ever a spring, and must put forth) to begin that course which some years past I purposed to travel, though I could now do it, not much disadvantageously. But I have some bridle upon me now more, more than then, by my marriage of this gentlewoman, in providing for whom I can and will show myself very honest, though not so fortunate.
    To seek preferment here with any but your Lordship were a madness.

---

1 At its final meeting each term, the High Commission reduced or remitted sentences it had imposed. Such a meeting took place on 25 February 1602.
2 See Letter I (note).

14

Every great man to whom I shall address any such suit will silently dispute the case and say, 'Would my Lord Keeper so disgraciously have imprisoned him and flung him away if he had not done some other great fault of which we hear not?' – so that to the burden of my true weaknesses I shall have this addition of a very prejudicial suspicion that I am worse than I hope your Lordship doth think me, or would that the world should think. I have therefore no way before me, but must turn back to your Lordship, who knows that redemption was no less work than creation.

I know my fault so well and so well acknowledge it that I protest I have not so much as inwardly grudged or startled at the punishment. I know your Lordship's disposition so well as, though in course of justice it be of proof against clamours of offenders, yet it is not strong enough to resist itself and I know itself naturally inclines it to pity. I know mine own necessity, out of which I humbly beg that your Lordship will so much entender your heart towards me as to give me leave to come into your presence. Affliction, misery and destruction are not there, and everywhere else where I am, they are.

Your Lordship's most poor and most penitent servant,

J. Donne

Letter X. *To Sir George More*   1 March 1602

Written on the same day as Letter IX, this letter shows that Donne realised the potential value of having Sir George as an ally. Possibly because he now felt that there was nothing to be gained from opposing the marriage, Sir George acceded to Donne's request to support his suit to Egerton, who was, however, deaf to both men's pleas. According to Izaak Walton, he refused to reinstate Donne on the grounds that 'it was inconsistent with his place and credit to discharge and readmit servants at the request of passionate petitioners'.

Sir,

If I could fear that in so much worthiness as is in you there were no mercy, or if these weights oppressed only my shoulders and my fortunes and not my conscience and hers whose good is dearer to me by much than my life, I should not thus trouble you with my letters. But when I see that this storm hath shaked me at root in my Lord's favour, where I was well planted, and have just reason to fear that those ill reports which malice hath raised of me may have troubled hers, I can leave no honest way untried to remedy these miseries, nor find any way more honest than this: out of an humble and repentant heart for the fault done to you, to beg both your pardon and assistance in my suit to my Lord.

I should wrong you as much again as I did if I should think you sought to destroy me, but though I be not headlongly destroyed, I languish and rust dangerously. From seeking preferments abroad, my love and conscience restrains me; from hoping for them here, my Lord's disgracings cut me off. My imprisonments and theirs whose love to me brought them to it hath already cost me £40.[1] And the love of my friends, though it be not utterly grounded upon my fortunes, yet I know suffers somewhat in these long and uncertain disgraces of mine.

I therefore humbly beseech you to have so charitable a pity of what I have and do and must suffer as to take to yourself the comfort of having saved from such destruction as your just anger might have laid upon him, a sorrowful and honest man. I was bold in my last letter to beg leave of you that I might write to your daughter. Though I understand thereupon that after the Thursday you were not displeased that I should, yet I have not nor will not without your knowledge do it. But now I beseech you that I may, since I protest before God it is the greatest of my afflictions not to do it. In all the world is not more true sorrow than in my heart, nor more understanding of true repentance than in yours, and therefore God, whose pardon in such cases is never denied, gives me leave to hope that you will favourably consider my necessities.

To his merciful guiding and protection I commend you, and cease to trouble you.

Yours in all humbleness and dutiful obedience,
J. Donne

---

1 Christopher Brooke, a friend of Donne's from his time at Lincoln's Inn, had given away the bride while his younger brother Samuel, a clergyman, had conducted the ceremony. Both Brookes had been imprisoned for their part in the proceedings.

Letter XI. *To Sir Henry Goodyer* 1604

The letters Donne wrote to Goodyer on a weekly basis, which form the core of his extant correspondence, take us as near as anything does to the real Donne. Here, in one of the earliest to have survived, he self-consciously distinguishes the kind of letter he writes from those to be found in existing collections. The final paragraph makes it clear that he and Goodyer were in the habit of exchanging prose 'problems' with each other. Goodyer evidently has, or has had, some of Donne's in his possession.

Sir,

If you were here, you would not think me importune if I bid you good morrow every day, and such a patience will excuse my often letters. No other kind of conveyance is better for knowledge or love. What treasures of moral knowledge are in Seneca's letters to only one Lucilius? And what of natural in Pliny's? How much of the story of the time is in Cicero's letters? And how all of these times in the Jesuits' eastern and western epistles? Where can we find so perfect a character of Phalaris as in his own letters, which are almost so many writs of execution, or of Brutus as in his private seals for money? The evangiles [gospels] and Acts [of the Apostles] teach us what to believe, but the epistles of the apostles what to do. And those who have endeavoured to dignify Seneca above his worth have no way fitter than to imagine letters between him and St Paul, as they think also that they have expressed an excellent person in that letter which they obtrude [conjecture] from our blessed Saviour to King Agabarus. The Italians, which are most discursive and think the world owes them all wisdom, abound so much in this kind of expressing that Michel Montaigne says he hath seen (as I remember) 400 volumes of Italian letters. But it is the other capacity which must make mine acceptable, that they are also the best conveyers of love.

But, though all knowledge be in those authors already, yet, as some poisons and some medicines hurt not nor profit except the creature in which they reside contribute their lively activities and vigour, so much of the knowledge buried in books perisheth and becomes ineffectual if it be not applied and refreshed by a companion or friend. Much of their goodness hath the same period which some physicians of Italy have observed to be in the biting of their tarantula, that it affects no longer than the fly lives. For with how much desire we read the papers of any living now (especially friends) which we would scarce allow a box in our cabinet or shelf in our library if they were dead? And we do justly in it, for the writings and words of men present we may examine, control [verify] and expostulate [debate], and receive satisfaction from the authors, but the other we must believe or discredit: they present no mean.

Since, then, at this time I am upon the stage, you may be content to hear me. And now that perchance I have brought you to it (as Thomas Badger did the King), now I have nothing to say. And it is well, for the letter is already long enough, else let this problem supply, which was occasioned by you, of women wearing stones, which (it seems) you were afraid women should read because you avert them at the beginning with a protestation of cleanliness. Martial found no way fitter to draw the Roman matrons to read one of his books, which he thinks most moral and cleanly, than to counsel them by the first epigram to skip the book because it was obscene. But either you write not at all for women or for those of sincerer palates. Though their unworthiness and your own ease be advocates for me with you, yet I must add my entreaty that you let go no copy of my Problems till I review them. If it be too late, at least be able to tell me who hath them.

Yours,
J. Donne

Letter XII. *To Sir Henry Goodyer*   1606

The subject of this letter of condolence is generally taken to be Goodyer's wife, who died in 1606, although she is not mentioned by name – and it seems as if there had been some ambiguity in the communication of the news of the death in question. Read as an attempt to console, the letter strikes a jarring note, but the intense self-absorption it displays, attractive or not, is typically Donnean.

Sir,

I live so far removed that even the ill news of your great loss (which is ever swiftest and loudest) found me not till now. Your letter speaks it not plain enough, but I am so accustomed to the worst that I am sure it is so in this. I am almost glad that I knew her so little, for I would have no more additions to sorrow. If I should comfort you, it were an alms acceptable in no other title than when poor give to poor, for I am more needy of it than you, and I know you well provided of Christian and learned and brave defences against all human accidents. I will make my best haste after your messenger; and if myself and the place had not been ill provided of horses, I had been the messenger, for you have taught me by granting more to deny no request.

Your honest, unprofitable friend,
J. Donne
Pyrford, 3 o'clock, just as yours came

Letter XIII. *To Sir Henry Goodyer*   January 1607

This letter is thought to refer to the birth of Donne's son Francis, baptised at Mitcham in Surrey in January 1607 and named after Sir Francis Wolley, who had offered the Donnes a home on his estate at Pyrford in the wake of Egerton's decision not to reinstate Donne as his secretary. (From there the Donnes had moved, in 1606, to a cottage at Mitcham, where they lived until the autumn of 1612.)

Sir,
    Though you escape my lifting up of your latch by removing, you cannot my letters. Yet of this letter I do not much accuse myself, for I serve your commandment in it, for it is only to convey to you this paper opposed to those with which you trusted me. It is (I cannot say the weightiest, but truly) the saddest lucubration and night's passage that ever I had. For it exercised those hours which, with extreme danger of her whom I should hardly have abstained from recompensing for her company in this world with accompanying her out of it, increased my poor family with a son. Though her anguish and my fears and hopes seem divers [numerous] and wild distractions from this small business of your papers, yet because they all narrowed themselves and met in *via regia* [the royal road], which is the consideration of ourselves and God, I thought it time not unfit for this dispatch. Thus much more than needed I have told you, whilst my fire was lighting at Tincomb's at ten o'clock.

Yours ever entirely,
J. Donne

Letter XIV. *To Sir Henry Goodyer*   March 1607

The most significant section of this self-deprecating letter is arguably the postscript, for it confirms what Walton says about Donne's intimacy at about this time with Thomas Morton, the Dean of Gloucester. Morton was busy writing prose tracts defending the Church of England against onslaughts from Rome, and it is quite possible that Donne was actively involved in their composition, perhaps working as Morton's research assistant.

Sir,
    Though my friendship be good for nothing else, it may give you the profit of a temptation or of an affliction. It may excuse [exercise?] your patience, and though it cannot allure, it shall importune you. Though I know you have many worthy friends of all ranks, yet I add something, since I, which am of none, would fain be your friend too. There is some of the honour and some of the degrees of a creation to make a friendship of nothing.
    Yet, not to annihilate myself utterly (for though it seem humbleness, yet it is a work of as much almightiness to bring a thing to nothing as from nothing), though I be not of the best stuff for friendship, which men of warm and durable fortunes only are, I cannot say that I am not of the best fashion, if truth and honesty be that which I must ever exercise towards you, because I learned it of you. For the conversation with worthy men and of good example, though it sow not virtue in us, yet produceth and ripeneth it.
    Your man's haste and mine to Mitcham cuts off this letter here, yet, as in little patterns torn from a whole piece, this may tell you what all I am. Though by taking me before my day, which I accounted Tuesday, I make short payment of this duty of letters, yet I have a little comfort in this, that you see me hereby willing to pay those debts which I can before my time.
                                        Your affectionate friend,
                                                    J. Donne

You forget to send me the *Apology*,[1] and many times I think it an injury to remember one of a promise lest it confess a distrust, but of the book, by occasion of reading the dean's answer to it, I have sometimes some want [need].

---

1 An anti-Protestant tract refuted by Morton.

Letter XV. *To Mrs Magdalen Herbert*   11 July 1607

Donne's relationship with Mrs Herbert was of great importance to him, and in about 1607 it was put on a surer footing when he became a frequent visitor at her London house. The exaggerated praise which he heaps upon her in this letter and the two following (printed as a group by Walton in his Life of Mr George Herbert*) typifies the tone of Donne's dealings with his female patrons, as does his insistence in this letter that he is not flattering his addressee.*

Madam,

Every excuse hath in it somewhat of accusation, and since I am innocent and yet must excuse, how shall I do for that part of accusing? By my troth, as deperate and perplexed men grow from thence bold, so must I take the boldness of accusing you, who would draw so dark a curtain betwixt me and your purposes as that I had no glimmering, neither of your goings nor the way which my letters might haunt. Yet I have given this licence to travel, but I know not whither, nor it. It is therefore rather a pinnace [small light vessel] to discover, and the entire colony of letters, of hundreds and fifties, must follow, whose employment is more honourable than that which our state meditates to Virginia, because you are worthier than all that country of which that is a wretched inch, for you have better treasure and a harmlessness. If this sound like a flattery, tear it out. I am to my letters as rigid a Puritan as Caesar was to his wife. I can as ill endure a suspicion and misinterpretable word as a fault. But remember that nothing is flattery which the speaker believes, and of the grossest flatteries there is this good use, that they tell us what we should be. But, madam, you are beyond instruction, and therefore there can belong to you only praise, of which, though you be no good hearer, yet allow all my letters leave to have in them one part of it, which is thankfulness towards you.

Your unworthiest servant, except your accepting have mended him,

John Donne
Mitcham

Letter XVI. *To Mrs Magdalen Herbert*   23 July 1607

Madam,

This is my second letter, in which, though I cannot tell you what is good, yet this is the worst, that I must be a great part of it. Yet to me, that is recompense because you must be mingled. After I knew you were gone (for I must little less than accusingly tell you, I knew not you would go), I sent my first letter, like a Bevis of Hampton, to seek adventures. This day I came to town, and to the best part of it: your house. For your memory is a state-cloth[1] and presence, which I reverence though you be away, though I need not seek that there which I have about and within me. There, though I found my accusation, yet anything to which your hand is is a pardon. Yet I would not burn my first letter because, as in great destiny no small passage can be omitted or frustrated, so in my resolution of writing almost daily to you I would have no link of the chain broke by me, both because my letters interpret one another and because only their number can give them weight.

If I had your commission and instructions to do you the service of a lieger [resident] ambassador here, I could say something of the Countess of Devon, of the States[2] and such things. But since to you, who are not only a world alone but the monarchy of the world yourself, nothing can be added, especially by me, I will sustain myself with the honour of being

Your servant extraordinary and without place,
John Donne
London

Letter XVII. *To Mrs Magdalen Herbert*   2 August 1607

Madam,

As we must die before we can have full glory and happiness, so before I can have this degree of it as to see you by a letter, I must also die, that is, come to London, to plaguy London, a place full of danger and vanity and vice, though the court be gone, and such it will be till your return redeem it. Not that the greatest virtue in the world, which is you, can be such a

---

1 The canopy which hung over the throne; like the throne, it was reverenced in the monarch's absence.
2 The Low Countries.

marshal as to defeat or disperse all the vice of this place. But as higher bodies remove or contract themselves when better come, so at your return we shall have one door open to innocence. Yet, madam, you are not such an Ireland as produceth neither ill nor good – no spiders nor nightingales, which is a rare degree of perfection. But you have found and practised that experiment, that even Nature out of her detesting of emptiness, if we will make that our work, to remove bad, will fill us with good things. To abstain from it was therefore but the childhood and minority of your soul, which hath been long exercised since in your manlier active part of doing good, of which, since I have been a witness and subject, not to tell you some-times that by your influence and example I have attained to such a step of goodness as to be thankful were both to accuse your power and judge-ment of impotency and infirmity.

Your Ladyship's in all services,
John Donne

Letter XVIII. *To Sir Henry Goodyer*   15 August 1607

Although many of Donne's letters communicate little tangible information, most contain at least one item of news, if only at the end or in a postscript: this letter's complete lack of informativeness, even on the subject of its writer, is unusual. (Perhaps it is this feature which causes Donne to be intrigued by the idea of his letters' permanence, which he thinks will enable Goodyer to reread them a year after they have been written.)

Sir,

In the history or style of friendship, which is best written both in deeds and words, a letter which is of a mixed nature and hath something of both is a mixed parenthesis. It may be left out, yet it contributes, though not to the being, yet to the verdure and freshness thereof. Letters have truly the same office as oaths. As these amongst light and empty men are but fill-ings and pauses and interjections, but with weightier they are sad attestations [serious testimonies], so are letters to some complement and obligation to others.

For mine, as I never authorised my servant to lie in my behalf (for if it were officious in him, it might be worse in me), so I allow my letters much less that civil dishonesty both because they go from me more considerately and because they are permanent, for in them I may speak to you in your chamber a year hence before I know not whom, and not hear myself. They shall, therefore, ever keep the sincerity and intemperateness of the fountain whence they are derived. And as wheresoever the leaves fall, the root is in my heart, so shall they, as that sucks good affections towards you there, have ever true impressions thereof.

Thus much information is in very leaves, that they can tell what the tree is, and these can tell you I am a friend and an honest man. Of what general use the fruit should speak, and I have none, and of what particular profit to you, your application and experimenting should tell you, and you can make none of such a nothing. Yet even of barren sycamores such as I, there were use, if either any light flashings or scorching vehemencies or sudden showers made you need so shadowy an example or remembrancer. But, sir, your fortune and mind do you this happy injury, that they make all kind of fruits useless unto you. Therefore I have placed my love wisely where I need communicate nothing. All this, though perchance you read it not till Michaelmas, was told you at

Mitcham

Letter XIX. *To Sir Henry Goodyer*   Summer 1607

This letter is unusually rich in references to what Donne has been writing: it mentions a verse letter, two more Problems (see Letter XI) and 'a rag of verses'. The latter are most likely to have been some of the Songs *and* Sonnets. *So dismissive-sounding a description of them may point to a desire on Donne's part to have them thought of as a fairly unimportant by-product of his leisure hours in an age when the writing of verse for publication tended to be frowned upon.*

Sir,

This Tuesday morning, which hath brought me to London, presents me with all your letters. Methought it was a rent day, I mean such as yours and not as mine – and yet such, too, when I considered how much I ought [owed] you for them, how good a mother, how fertile and abundant the understanding is if she have a good father, and how well friendship performs that office. For that which is denied in other generations is done in this of yours, for here is superfetation [a second conception], child upon child, and that which is more strange, twins at a later conception.

If in my second religion, friendship, I had a conscience, either *errantem*, to mistake good and bad and indifferent, or *opinantem*, to be ravished by other's opinions or examples, or *dubiam*, to adhere to neither part, or *scrupulosam*, to incline to one but upon reasons light in themselves or indiscussed in me (which are almost all the diseases of conscience), I might mistake your often, long and busy letters and fear you did but entreat me to have mercy upon you and spare you. For you know our court took the resolution that it was the best way to dispatch the French prince back again quickly to receive him solemnly, ceremoniously and expensively when he hoped a domestic and durable entertainment.

I never meant to excel you in weight nor price, but in number and bulk I thought I might because he may cast up a greater sum who hath but forty small moneys than he with twenty portugueses. The memory of friends (I mean only for letters) neither enters ordinarily into busied men, because they are ever employed within, nor into men of pleasure, because they are never at home. For these wishes, therefore, which you won out of your pleasure and recreation, you were as excusable to me if you writ seldom as Sir Henry Wotton is, under the oppression of business or the necessity of seeming so, or more than he because I hope you have both pleasure and business. Only to me, who have neither, this omission were sin, for though writing be not of the precepts of friendship but of the counsels, yet, as in some cases to some men counsels become precepts, and though not immediately from God, yet very roundly and quickly from his Church (as selling and dividing goods in the first time, continence in the Roman Church and order and decency in ours), so to me who can do nothing else, it seems to bind my conscience to write, and it is sin to do against the conscience, though that err.

Yet no man's letters might be better wanted [missed] than mine since my whole letter is nothing else but a confession that I should and would write. I owed you a letter in verse before by mine own promise, and now that you think you have hedged in that debt by a greater, by your letter in verse, I think it now most seasonable and fashionable for me to break. At least to write presently were to accuse myself of not having read yours so often as such a letter deserves from you to me.

To make my debt greater (for such is the desire of all who cannot or mean not to pay), I pray, read these two Problems, for such light flashes as these have been my hawkings in my sorry journeys. I accompany them with another rag of verses, worthy of that name for the smallness and age, for it hath lain long among my other papers and laughs at them that have adventured to you, for I think till now you saw it not, and neither you nor it should repent it. Sir, if I were anything, my love to you might multiply it and dignify it, but infinite nothings are but one such. Yet, since even chimeras have some name and titles, I am also

Yours.

Letter XX. *To Mrs Magdalen Herbert*   Summer 1607?

Walton prints this letter to illustrate how the relationship between Donne and Mrs Herbert, though very warm, was not 'an amity that polluted their souls'. (The letter's tone is noticeably more serious than that of Letters XV to XVII.)

The 'holy hymns and sonnets' Donne is sending were probably his sonnet sequence La Corona; *the 'enclosed sonnet' was that beginning 'Her of your name', printed with* La Corona *in modern editions of Donne's verse.*

Madam,

Your favours to me are everywhere. I use them and have them. I enjoy them at London and leave them there, and yet find them at Mitcham. Such riddles as these become things unexpressible, and such is your goodness. I was almost sorry to find your servant here this day because I was loath to have any witness of my not coming home last night, and, indeed, of my coming this morning. But my not coming was excusable because earnest business detained me, and my coming this day is by the example of your St Mary Magdalen, who rose early upon Sunday to seek that which she loved most – and so did I. And from her and myself I return such thanks as are due to one to whom we owe all the good opinion that they whom we need most have of us. By this messenger, and on this good day, I commit the enclosed holy hymns and sonnets (which for the matter, not the workmanship, have yet escaped the fire) to your judgement, and to your protection, too, if you think them worthy of it, and I have appointed this enclosed sonnet to usher them to your happy hand.

Your unworthiest servant, unless your accepting him have mended him

John Donne
Mitcham

Letter XXI. *To Sir Henry Goodyer*   9 October 1607

This letter, the opening of which is likely to put readers of the Songs *and* Sonnets *in mind of 'The Ecstasy', gives a good idea of the range of Donne's religious, philosophical and scientific interests. His critical stance on sectarian wrangling and fierce disdain of what he calls 'positive and dogmatical truths which are not worthy of that dignity' anticipate recurrent strains in his sermons.*

Sir,

I make account that this writing of letters, when it is with any seriousness, is a kind of ecstasy and a departure and secession [temporary migration] and suspension of the soul, which doth then communicate itself to two bodies. And, as I would every day provide for my soul's last convoy though I know not when I shall die (and perchance I shall never die),[1] so for these ecstasies in letters, I oftentimes deliver myself over in writing when I know not when those letters shall be sent to you, and many times they never are, for I have a little satisfaction in seeing a letter written to you upon my table though I meet no opportunity of sending it.

Especially this summer when, either by my early retiring home or your irresolutions of your own purposes or some other possessions [ideas] of yours, you did less reveal to me your progresses and stations [halts] and where I might cross you by letters than heretofore, I make shift to lay little fault upon you because my pardon might be easier if I transgress into a longer and busier letter than your country sports admit. But you may read it in winter, and by that time I may more clearly express myself for those things which have entered into me concerning your soul. For as the greatest advantage which man's soul is thought to have beyond others is that which they call *actum reflexum* and *iteratum* [the act of reflection and repeated reflection] (for beasts do the same things as we do, but yet they do not consider nor remember the circumstances and inducements, and by what power and faculty it is that they do them), so of those which they call *actum reflexum* the noblest is that which reflects upon the soul itself, and considers and meditates it. Into which consideration, when I walk after my slow and unperfect pace, I begin to think that, as litigious men tired with suits admit any arbitrement [compromise], and princes travailed [wearied] with long and wasteful war descend to such conditions of peace as they are soon after

---

1 Alluding to the possibility that the second coming of Christ might occur during Donne's lifetime.

ashamed to have embraced, so philosophers and so all sects of Christians, after long disputations and controversies, have allowed many things for positive and dogmatical truths which are not worthy of that dignity. And so many doctrines have grown to be the ordinary diet and food of our spirits and have place in the pap of catechisms which were admitted but as physic [medicine] in that present distemper [disease] or accepted in a lazy weariness when men, so they might have something to rely upon, and to excuse themselves from more painful inquisition, never examined what that was. To which indisposition of ours the casuists are so indulgent as that they allow a conscience to adhere to any probable opinion against a more probable and do never bind him to seek out which is the more probable, but give him leave to dissemble it and to depart from it, if by mischance he come to know it. This, as it appears in all sciences, so most manifestly in physic, which for a long time considering nothing but plain curing, and that but by example and precedent, the world at last longed for some certain canons and rules how these cures might be accomplished. And when men are inflamed with this desire and that such a fire breaks out that rages and consumes infinitely by heat of argument except some of authority interpose.[2] This produced Hippocrates his aphorisms, and the world slumbered or took breath in his resolution divers [several] hundreds of years. And then in Galen's time, which was not satisfied with the effect of curing nor with the knowledge how to cure, broke out another desire of finding out the causes why those simples [medicines] wrought those effects. Then Galen, rather to stay their stomachs [satisfy their appetites] than that he gave them enough, taught them the qualities of the four elements, and arrested them upon this, that all differences of qualities proceeded from them. And after (not much before our time), men perceiving that all effects in physic could not be derived from these beggarly and impotent properties of the elements, and that therefore they were driven often to that miserable refuge of specific form and of antipathy and sympathy, we see the world hath turned upon new principles which are attributed to Paracelsus, but, indeed, too much to his honour.

Certainly it is also so in the physic of our soul, divinity, for in the primitive Church, when amongst the Fathers there were so divers [many different] opinions of the state of the soul presently after this life, they easily inclined to be content to do as much for them dead as when they were alive, and so concurred in a charitable disposition to pray for them, which

---

2   This sentence is clearly defective, but the gist is clear.

manner of prayer then in use no Christian Church at this day, having received better light, will allow of [accept as valid], so also, when in the beginning of St Augustine's time grace had been so much advanced that man's nature was scarce admitted to be so much as any means or instrument (not only no kind of cause) of his own good works. And soon after, in St Augustine's time also, man's free will (by fierce opposition and arguing against the former error) was too much overvalued, and admitted into too near degrees of fellowship with grace, those times admitted a doctrine and form of reconciliation which, though for reverence to the time, both the Dominicans and Jesuits at this day in their great quarrel about grace and free will would yet seem to maintain, yet indifferent and dispassioned men of that Church see there is no possibility in it, and therefore accuse it of absurdity and almost of heresy.

I think it falls out thus also in the matter of the soul. For Christian religion, presuming a soul and intending principally her happiness in the life to come, hath been content to accept any way which hath been obtruded [conjectured] how this soul is begun in us. Hence it is that whole Christian Churches arrest themselves upon propagation from parents, and other whole Christian Churches allow only infusion from God, in both which opinions there appear such infirmities as it is time to look for a better. For whosoever will adhere to the way of propagation can never evict [prove] necessarily and certainly a natural immortality in the soul if the soul result out of matter, nor shall he ever prove that all mankind hath any more than one soul, as certainly of all beasts, if they receive such souls as they have from their parents, every species can have but one soul. And they which follow the opinion of infusion from God and of a new creation (which is now the more common opinion), as they can very hardly defend the doctrine of original sin (the soul is forced to take this infection and comes not into the body of her own disposition), so shall they never be able to prove that all those whom we see in the shape of men have an immortal and reasonable soul because our parents are as able as any other species is to give us a soul of growth and of sense and to perform all vital and animal functions, and so without infusion of such a soul may produce a creature as wise and well disposed as any horse or elephant, of which degree many whom we see come far short. Nor hath God bound or declared himself that he will always create a soul for every embryon. There is yet therefore no opinion in philosophy nor divinity so well established as constrains us to believe both that the soul is immortal and that every particular man hath such a soul – which, since out of the great mercy of our God we do constantly believe, I am ashamed that we do not also know it by searching further.

But as sometimes we had rather believe a traveller's lie than go to disprove him, so men rather cleave to these ways than seek new. Yet because I have meditated therein, I will shortly acquaint you with what I think, for I would not be in danger of that law of Moses, that if a man dig a pit and cover it not, he must recompense those which are damnified [injured] by it, which is often interpreted of such as shake old opinions and do not establish new as certain, but leave consciences in a worse danger than they found them in. I believe that law of Moses hath in it some mystery and appliableness, for by that law men are only then bound to that indemnity and compensation if an ox or an ass (that is, such as are of a strong constitution and accustomed to labour) fall therein, but it is not said so if a sheep or a goat fall. No more are we, if men in a silliness or wantonness will stumble or take a scandal, bound to rectify them at all times. And, therefore, because I justly presume you strong and watchful enough, I make account that I am not obnoxious [answerable] to that law since my meditations are neither too wide nor too deep for you, except only that my way of expressing them may be extended beyond your patience and pardon, which I will therefore tempt no longer at this time.

Your very affectionate friend and servant and lover,
J. Donne
From Mitcham, my close prison ever since I saw you

Letter XXII. *To Sir Henry Goodyer*   March 1608

This shares some of Letter XXI's concerns, as well as offering additional insights into Donne's state of mind during the Mitcham years. It also shows a preoccupation with another topic of perennial fascination for him, the nature of knowledge, especially self-knowledge: the letters from this period suggest that leisure for reflection greatly encouraged Donne's propensity for self-examination.

Sir,

I hope you are now welcome to London, and well, and well comforted in your father's health and love, and well contented that we ask you how you do and tell you how we are, which yet I cannot of myself. If I knew that I were ill, I were well, for we consist of three parts, a soul, and body and mind, which I call those thoughts and affections and passions which neither soul nor body hath alone but have been begotten by their communication, as music results out of our breath and a cornet. And of all these the diseases are cures, if they be known. Of our souls' sicknesses, which are sins, the knowledge is to acknowledge, and that is her physic [medicine], in which we are not dieted by drams and scruples [small divisions of weight], for we cannot take too much. Of our body's infirmities, though our knowledge be partly *ab extrinseco* [gained externally] from the opinion of the physician and that the subject and matter be flexible and various, yet their rules are certain, and if the matter be rightly applied to the rule, our knowledge thereof is also certain.

But of the diseases of the mind there is no criterion, no canon, no rule. For our own taste and apprehension and interpretation should be the judge, and that is the disease itself. Therefore, sometimes when I find myself transported with jollity and love of company, I hang leads at my heels and reduce to my thoughts my fortunes, my years, the duties of a man, of a friend, of a husband, of a father, and all the incumbencies [burdens] of a family. When sadness dejects me, either I countermine it with another sadness or I kindle squibs [fireworks] about me again and fly into sportfulness and company, and I find ever after all that I am like an exorcist which had long laboured about one which at last appears to have the mother [hysteria], that I still [always] mistake my disease. And I still vex myself with this because, if I know it not, nobody can know it. And I comfort myself because I see dispassioned men are subject to the like ignorances. For divers [different] minds out of the same thing often draw contrary conclusions, as Augustine thought devout Antony to be therefore full of the Holy Ghost because, not being able to read, he could say the whole Bible and interpret it, and Thyreus the Jesuit, for the same reason, doth think all the Anabaptists to be possessed. And as often out of contrary things men draw one conclusion.

As to the Roman Church magnificence and splendour hath ever been an argument of God's favour, and poverty and affliction to the Greek, out of this variety of minds it proceeds that, though our souls would go to one end, heaven, and all our bodies must go to one end, the earth, yet our third part, the mind, which is our natural guide here, chooses to every man a several [individual] way. Scarce any man likes what another doth, nor, advisedly, that which himself.

But, sir, I am beyond my purpose. I mean to write a letter, and I am fallen into a discourse, and I do not only take you from some business but I make you a new business by drawing you into these meditations, in which let my openness be an argument of such love as I would fain express in some worthier fashion.

Letter XXIII. *To Sir Henry Goodyer*   Spring 1608

Reading this melancholy letter alongside the previous two, especially Letter XXII,
enables us to appreciate the mood swings to which Donne was particularly suscep-
tible during this period of his life when he had no regular employment and was,
much of the time, cut off from the kinds of society and activities he really enjoyed.
What seems to alleviate his bleak mood somewhat is sharing his 'meditations' with
Goodyer.

Sir,
    Because I am in a place and season where I see everything bud forth, I
must do so too, and vent some of my meditations to you, the rather
because, all other buds being yet without taste or virtue, my letters may
be like them. The pleasantness of the season displeases me. Everything
refreshes, and I wither, and I grow older and not better. My strength diminishes, and my load grows and, being to pass more and more storms, I find
that I have not only cast out all my ballast which nature and time gives
(reason and discretion), and so am as empty and light as vanity can make
me, but I have over-fraught myself with vice, and so am riddingly[1] subject
to two contrary wracks, sinking and oversetting, and under the iniquity of
such a disease as enforces the patient, when he is almost starved, not only
to fast but to purge. For I have much to take in and much to cast out.
Sometimes I think it easier to discharge myself of vice than of vanity, as
one may sooner carry the fire out of a room than the smoke, and then I
see it was a new vanity to think so. And when I think sometimes that
vanity, because it is thin and airy, may be expelled with virtue or business
or substantial vice, I find that I give entrance thereby to new vices.
    Certainly, as the earth and water, one sad, the other fluid, make but one
body, so to air and vanity there is but one *centrum morbi* [centre of the
disease], and that which later physicians say of our bodies is fitter for our
minds. For that which they call destruction, which is a corruption and want
of those fundamental parts whereof we consist, is vice, and that *collectio ster-*
corum [dungheap], which is but the excrement of that corruption, is our
vanity and indiscretion. Both these have but one root in me, and must be
pulled out at once, or never. But I am so far from digging to it that I know

---

1 Perhaps a misprint for 'riddlingly' (that is, in a riddling or perplexing manner).

not where it is, for it is not in mine eyes only but in every sense, nor in my concupiscence only but in every power and affection.

Sir, I was willing to let you see how impotent a man you love, not to dishearten you from doing so still (for my vices are not infectious nor wandering; they came not yesterday, nor mean to go away today: they inn [make a short stay] not, but dwell in me, and see themselves so welcome and find in me so good bad company of one another that they will not change, especially to one not apprehensive nor easily accessible), but I do it that your counsel might cure me and, if you deny that, your example shall, for I will as much strive to be like you as I will wish you to continue good.

Letter XXIV. *To Sir Henry Goodyer*   September 1608

As well as providing a vivid account (all too rare in his extant correspondence) of Donne's domestic circumstances, this letter serves as a warning against exaggerating the extent of his isolation from polite society during the Mitcham years: he is clearly still a part of it despite his fear that his lifestyle may cause him to 'melt into a melancholy'. The letter also contains the earliest reference in this collection to Donne's friend and patron, Lucy, Countess of Bedford.

Sir,

I write not to you out of my poor library, where to cast mine eye upon good authors kindles or refreshes sometimes meditations not unfit to communicate to near friends, nor from the highway, where I am contracted and inverted into myself, which are my two ordinary forges of letters to you, but I write from the fireside in my parlour and in the noise of three gamesome children and by the side of her whom, because I have transplanted into a wretched fortune, I must labour to disguise that from her by all such honest devices as giving her my company and discourse. Therefore I steal from her all the time which I give this letter and it is therefore that I take so short a list [run-up] and gallop so fast over it. I have not been out of my house since I received your packet.

As I have much quenched my senses and disused my body from pleasure, and so tried how I can endure to be mine own grave, so I try now how I can suffer a prison. And since it is but to build one wall more about our soul, she is still in her own centre, how many circumstances soever fortune or our own perverseness cast about her. I would I could as well entreat her to go out as she knows whither to go.

But if I melt into a melancholy whilst I write, I shall be taken in the manner, and I sit by one too tender towards these impressions, and it is so much our duty to avoid all occasions of giving them sad apprehensions, as St Jerome accuses Adam of no other fault in eating the apple but that he did it *ne contristaretur delicias suas* [so as not to mix his pleasures with sadness]. I am not careful what I write because the enclosed letters may dignify this ill-favoured bark, and they need not grudge so coarse a countenance because they are now to accompany themselves. My man fetched them, and therefore I can say no more of them than themselves say. Mistress Meautys entreated me by her letter to hasten hers – as I think, for by my troth I cannot read it. My Lady was dispatching in so much haste for Twickenham as she gave no word to a letter which I sent with yours. Of Sir Thomas Bartlett I can say nothing, nor of the plague, though your letter bid me, but that he diminishes, the other increases, but in what proportion I am not clear. To them at Hammersmith and Mistress Herbert, I will do your command. If I have been good in hope or can promise any little offices in the future probably, it is comfortable, for I am the worst present man in the world. Yet the instant, though it be nothing, joins times together, and therefore this unprofitableness, since I have been and will still [always] endeavour to be so, shall not interrupt me now from being

Your servant and lover,
J. Donne

Letter XXV. *To Sir Henry Goodyer* September 1608

The deep-seated preoccupation with death and dying evident in this letter was accentuated during Donne's extended period of partial exile from court life by his sense of having irreparably damaged his prospects. His perception of the futility of his existence was heightened once again by his acute awareness of his lack of fixed employment (see Letter XXIII), the importance of which would become a frequent burden of his sermons.

Sir,

Every Tuesday I make account that I turn a great hour-glass and consider that a week's life is run out since I writ. But if I ask myself what I have done in the last watch or would do in the next, I can say nothing. If I say that I have passed it without hurting any, so may the spider in my window. The primitive monks were excusable in their retirings and enclosures of themselves, for even of them every one cultivated his own garden and orchard, that is, his soul and body, by meditation and manufactures, and they ought [owed] the world no more since they consumed none of her sweetness, nor begot others to burden her. But for me, if I were able to husband all my time so thriftily as not only not to wound my soul in any minute by actual sin, but not to rob and cozen [cheat] her by giving any part to pleasure or business, but bestow it all upon her in meditation, yet even in that I should wound her more and contract another guiltiness, as the eagle were very unnatural if, because she is able to do it, she should perch a whole day upon a tree, staring in contemplation of the majesty and glory of the sun, and let her young eaglets starve in the nest.

Two of the most precious things which God hath afforded us here for the agony and exercise of our sense and spirit, which are a thirst and inhiation [greedy desire] after the next life and a frequency of prayer and meditation in this, are often envenomed and putrefied, and stray into a corrupt disease. For as God doth thus occasion and positively concur to evil, that when a man is purposed to do a great sin, God infuses some good thoughts which make him choose a less sin or leave out some circumstance which aggravated that, so the Devil doth not only suffer but provoke us to some things naturally good upon condition that we shall omit some other more necessary and more obligatory. And this is his greatest subtlety, because herein we have the deceitful comfort of having done well, and can very hardly spy our error because it is but an insensible omission and no accusing act. With the first of these I have often suspected myself to be overtaken, which is with a desire of the next life, which, though I know it is not merely out of a weariness of this (because I had the same desires when I went with the tide and enjoyed fairer hopes than now), yet I doubt [suspect] worldly encumbrances have increased it.

I would not that death should take me asleep. I would not have him merely seize me and only declare me to be dead, but win me and overcome me. When I must shipwreck, I would do it in a sea, where mine impotency might have some excuse, not in a sullen, weedy lake, where I could not have so much as exercise for my swimming. Therefore, I would fain do something, but that I cannot tell what is no wonder. For to choose is to do, but to be no part of any body is to be nothing. At most the greatest persons are but great wens [warts] and excrescences [growths], men of wit and delightful conversation but as moles for ornament, except they be so

35

incorporated into the body of the world that they contribute something to the sustentation [maintenance] of the whole.

This I made account that I begun early when I understood[1] the study of our laws, but was diverted by the worst voluptuousness, which is an hydroptic [insatiable], immoderate desire of humane learning and languages, beautiful ornaments to great fortunes, but mine needed an occupation and a course, which I thought I entered well into when I submitted myself to such a service as I thought might have employed those poor advantages which I had. And there I stumbled, too,[2] yet I would try again, for to this hour I am nothing, or so little that I am scarce subject and argument good enough for one of mine own letters. Yet I fear that doth not ever proceed from a good root that I am so well content to be less – that is, dead. You, sir, are far enough from these descents. Your virtue keeps you secure and your natural disposition to mirth will preserve you. But loose none of these holds. A slip is often as dangerous as a bruise, and though you cannot fall to my lowness, yet in a much less distraction you may meet my sadness. For he is no safer which falls from an high tower into the leads than he which falls from thence to the ground. Make therefore to yourself some mark and go towards it *allègrement* [cheerfully]. Though I be in such a planetary and erratic fortune that I can do nothing constantly, yet you may find some constancy in my constant advising you to it.

Your hearty true friend,
J. Donne

I came this evening from Mr Jones his house in Essex, where Mr Martin hath been and left a relation [account] of Captain Whitlock's death. Perchance it is no news to you, but it was to me. Without doubt want broke him, for when Mr Holland's company (by reason of the plague) broke, the captain sought to be at Mrs Jones's house, who in her husband's absence declining it, he went in the night, his boy carrying his cloak-bag, on foot to the Lord of Sussex, who, going next day to hunt, the captain not then sick, told him he would see him no more. A chaplain came up to him, to whom he delivered an account of his understanding and, I hope, of his belief, and soon after died, and my Lord hath buried him with his own ancestors. Perchance his life needed a longer sickness, but a man may go faster and safer when he enjoys that daylight of a clear and sound under-

---

1 Probably a misprint for 'undertook'.
2 Presumably by his clandestine marriage.

standing than in the night or twilight of an ague or other disease. And the grace of Almighty God doth everything suddenly and hastily but depart from us: it enlightens us, warms us, heats us, ravishes us at once. Such a medicine, I fear, his inconsideration needed, and I hope as confidently that he had it. As our soul is infused when it is created, and created when it is infused, so at her going out God's mercy is had by asking, and that is asked by having. Lest your Polesworth carrier should cozen [trick] me, I send my man with this letter early to London, whither this Tuesday all the court come to a christening at Arundel House, and stay in town so that I will sup with the good Lady, and write again tomorrow to you if anything be occasioned there which concerns you, and I will tell her so. Next day they are to return to Hampton, and upon Friday the King to Royston.

Letter XXVI. *To Sir Henry Goodyer*   Autumn 1608

References in Donne's correspondence to the precise circumstances and thinking underlying his poetry are very rare, and the description of the genesis of 'A Litany' in this letter greatly assists with explicating this important poem. (Donne was articulating an unusually conciliatory attitude to the Catholic Church at about the same time that he was engaged in the writing of anti-Catholic propaganda.)

Sir,
      This letter hath more merit than one of more diligence for I wrote it in my bed, and with much pain. I have occasion to sit late some nights in my study (which your books make a pretty library) and now I find that that room hath a wholesome emblematic use for, having under it a vault, I make that promise me that I shall die reading since my book and a grave are so near. But it hath another unwholesomeness, that by raw vapours rising from thence (for I can impute it to nothing else) I have contracted a sickness which I cannot name or describe, for it hath so much of a continual cramp that it wrests the sinews, so much of a tetany [lockjaw] that it withdraws and pulls the mouth, and so much of the gout (which they whose counsel I use say it is) that it is not like to be cured, though I am too hasty in three days to pronounce it.
      If it be the gout, I am miserable, for that affects dangerous parts as my neck and breast and (I think fearfully) my stomach, but it will not kill me

37

yet. I shall be in this world like a porter in a great house, ever nearest the door but seldomest abroad. I shall have many things to make me weary, and yet not get leave to be gone. If I go, I will provide by my best means that you suffer not for me in your bonds.[1] The estate which I should leave behind me of any estimation is my poor fame in the memory of my friends, and therefore I would be curious [careful] of it and provide that they repent not to have loved me.

Since my imprisonment in my bed I have made a meditation in verse, which I call 'A Litany'. The word, you know, imports no other than 'supplication', but all Churches have one form of supplication by that name. Amongst ancient annals, I mean some 800 years, I have met two litanies in Latin verse which gave me not the reason of my meditations, for in good faith I thought not upon them then, but they give me a defence if any man to a layman and a private impute it as a fault to take such divine and public names to his own little thoughts. The first of these was made by Ratpertus, a monk of Suevia, and the other by St Notker, of whom I will give you this note by the way, that he is a private saint for a few parishes. They were both but monks, and the litanies poor and barbarous enough, yet Pope Nicholas V valued their devotion so much that he canonised both their poems and commanded them for public service in their churches. Mine is for lesser chapels, which are my friends, and though a copy of it were due to you now, yet I am so unable to serve myself with writing it for you at this time (being some thirty staves [stanzas] of nine lines) that I must entreat you to take a promise that you shall have the first for a testimony of that duty which I owe to your love and to myself, who am bound to cherish it by my best offices. That by which it will deserve best acceptation is that neither the Roman Church need call it defective because it abhors not the particular mention of the blessed triumphers in heaven, nor the Reformed can discreetly accuse it of attributing more than rectified devotion ought to do.[2]

The day before I lay down, I was at London, where I delivered your letter for Sir Edward Conway and received another for you with the copy of my book,[3] of which it is impossible for me to give you a copy so soon

---

1 Goodyer had evidently taken over some responsibility for Donne's debts.
2 Donne hopes both that Catholic readers will be pleased with the poem's references to the saints and that Protestants will note that the saints are not asked to make intercession (a Catholic notion).
3 Probably Donne's treatise on suicide, *Biathanatos*.

for it is not of much less than 300 pages. If I die, it shall come to you in that fashion that your letter desires it. If I warm again (as I have often seen such beggars as my indisposition is end themselves soon, and the patient as soon), you and I shall speak together of that before it be too late to serve you in that commandment. At this time I only assure you that I have not appointed it upon any person nor ever purposed to print it, which later perchance you thought and grounded your request thereupon. A gentleman that visited me yesterday told me that our Church hath lost Mr Hugh Broughton, who is gone to the Roman side. I have known before that Serarius the Jesuit was an instrument from Cardinal Baronius to draw him to Rome to accept a stipend only to serve the Christian Churches in controversies with the Jews without endangering himself to change of his persuasion in particular deductions [points of debate] between these Christian Churches, or being enquired of or tempted thereunto, and I hope he is no otherwise departed from us. If he be, we shall not escape scandal in it because, though he be a man of many distempers [mood swings], yet when he shall come to eat assured bread and to be removed from partialities to which want drove him to make himself a reputation and raise up favourers, you shall see in that course of opposing the Jews he will produce worthy things, and our Church will perchance blush to have lost a soldier fit for that great battle and to cherish only those single duelisms [duels] between Rome and England or that more single and almost self-homicide between the unconformed [nonconformist] ministers and bishops. I writ to you last week that the plague increased, by which you may see that my letters [the text is defective at this point] opinion of the song, not that I make such trifles for praise, but because, as long as you speak comparatively of it with mine own and not absolutely, so long I am of your opinion even at this time when, I humbly thank God, I ask, and have, his comfort of sadder meditations. I do not condemn in myself that I have given my wit such evaporations as those if they be free from profaneness or obscene provocations.

Sir, you would pity me if you saw me write, and therefore will pardon me if I write no more. My pain hath drawn my head so much awry and holds it so that mine eye cannot follow mine hand. I receive you therefore into my prayers with mine own weary soul, and commend myself to yours. I doubt not but next week I shall be good news to you, for I have mending or dying on my side, which is two to one. If I continue thus, I shall have comfort in this, that my blessed Saviour, exercising his justice upon my two worldy parts, my fortune and my body, reserves all his mercy for that which best tastes it and most needs it: my soul. I profess to you truly that my loathness to give over now seems to myself an ill sign that I shall write no more.

Your poor friend and God's poor patient,

Jo. Donne

Letter XXVII. *To Lord Hay*   November 1608

Donne realised that James Hay had the potential to be of enormous use to him on account of his intimacy with the King. This letter, written while he was waiting to hear whether Hay had been successful in recommending him for a vacant secretary-ship in Ireland, shows us Donne at his most sycophantic. At the same time he can barely conceal how desperate he is to know whether Hay has heard anything.

Noblest Lord,

Ever to good ends the way and passage is fair and delightful, of which no man can have had a better experience than I, who for my best end, pretending to his Majesty's service, have by the way the honour to be received into your care. And though my fortune and my poor reputation importune me still [always] not to forsake myself but endeavour to be something, yet this descent of your Lordship and your taking knowledge of so unuseful a servant as I am gives me contentment and satisfaction enough and, so I may be sure to hold that room which your Lordship affords me in yourself, I care not to be anything else. It shall be my care that no fault make me unworthy of your Lordship's favour since I feel already that it is your Lordship's care to remove me from this darkness, in which my affection to do your Lordship service can no way appear.

I perceive not yet any purpose to make any successor in that place in Ireland. If any be made, and not I, this would be the worst degree of the ill fortune in that fail, that as I fear I should lose my hold in your Lordship, for it was but your affection that admitted me into you, but then your judgement would examine me and conclude me to be very unfit for you if I be not fit for Ireland. Now your Lordship knows all my hopes and fears, and it is in your power to make my destiny since to live in your memory is advancement enough, and I shall by your Lordship's favour be bold to refresh by my often letters, not as diffident solicitors from me but as your Lordship's auditors to bring you in the poor tribute of my thankfulness, who am, etc.

Letter XXVIII. *To Lord Hay*   Late 1608

This letter betrays Donne's frustration at the fact that when Hay urged James to appoint Donne to a secretaryship (see Letter XXVII), his marriage was found to count against him. This must have been especially galling since More and Egerton, to whom Donne invites Hay to apply for a reference, had long since been prepared to overlook his past conduct. The strength of Donne's flattery here reflects his fear that Hay may be about to abandon him.

Noblest Lord,

The same conscience [consciousness] of mine own unworthiness which kept me so long from daring to put myself into your Lordship's sight provokes me to write now. We are ever justly most tender and jealous of those things to which we have weakest title, and therefore, finding how little pretence I have to your Lordship's favour, I am not only diligent but curious [anxious] not to forfeit it. I have been told that when your Lordship did me that extreme favour of presenting my name, his Majesty remembered me by the worst part of my history, which was my disorderly proceedings seven years since in my nonage. As your Lordship's earnestness and alacrity in doing good and almost unthriftiness in multiplying and heaping your favours gave me scarce leisure to consider how great your first favour of promising was because you overtook it presently with a greater, which was the performing it, so I humbly beseech your Lordship to add another to these, not to be too apprehensive of any suspicion that there lies upon me any dishonourable stain or can make my King have any prejudice against me for that intemperate and hasty act of mine. For the Lord Chancellor[1] and his brother-in-law Sir George More, whose daughter I married, would both be likely, and will be ready to declare it, for his Majesty's satisfaction or your Lordship's, that their displeasure, commenced so long since, should not be thought to continue still or interrupt any of my fortunes. This I say lest I might have seemed to have betrayed your Lordship, and lest my ill fortune, by having got many victories upon myself, should dare to reach at your Lordship and think to work upon your constancy and perseverance in doing good by making you repent your own act in favouring me.

---

1 Sir Thomas Egerton.

41

I am, my Lord, somewhat more worthy of your favour than I was at first because every degree of your Lordship's favour is a great dignity. I am therefore in much confidence that your Lordship, which disdained me not then, will at least allow your own work in me and, as you have laid a foundation, so you will, by preferring me still [always] in your good opinion, build me up to such a capacity and worthiness as may be fit for your Lordship to dwell in, to which I only bring an honest and entire devotion to do your Lordship service. All the rest is your Lordship's work, whose hand I humbly kiss, and beg a pardon for saluting your Lordship herein by so bold a way as writing.

Letter XXIX. *To Sir Henry Goodyer*   May/June 1609

This somewhat sad letter with its description of Donne's books as dependable companions and of his cottage as 'a little thin house' has an important postscript: the Colloquy of Poissy *(1561) was an attempt to achieve harmony between French Catholics and Calvinists; Donne's longing for an eirenical book published at the time of the colloquy testifies to the interest in the reunification of Christendom implied in a number of the letters dating from 1608–9 (see, for example, Letter XXX).*

Sir,

Because things be conserved by the same means which established them, I nurse that friendship by letters which you begot so, though you have since strengthened it by more solid aliment [nourishment] and real offices. In these letters from the country there is this merit, that I do otherwse unwillingly turn mine eye or thoughts from my books, companions in whom there is no falsehood nor frowardness [perverseness], which words I am glad to observe that the holy authors often join as expressers and relatives to one other because else out of a natural descent to that unworthy fault of frowardness, furthered with that incommodity of a little thin house, I should have mistaken it to be a small thing which now I see equalled with the worst.

If you have laid my papers and books by, I pray let this messenger have them: I have determined upon them. If you have not, be content to do it in the next three or four days. So, sir, I kiss your hands and deliver to you an entire and clear [pure] heart, which shall ever when I am with you be in my face and tongue, and when I am from you, in my letters, for I will never draw curtain between you and it.

Yours very affectionately,

J. Donne

From your house at Mitcham. Friday morning

When you are sometimes at Mr Sackville's, I pray, ask if he have this book: Baldvinus' *De officio pii hominis in controversiis*.[1] It was written at the conference at Poissy, where Beza was, and he answered it. I long for it.

Letter XXX. *To Sir Henry Goodyer*   May/June 1609

Donne's description here of the Churches of England and Rome as 'sister teats of [God's] graces' is evidence of his remarkable independence of thought; he realised that such views were unusual at the time for he cautions Goodyer about the dangers of indiscretion. His enquiry as to whether it would be proper for him to accede to Goodyer's suggestion and write a poem for a potential new patron, the Countess of Huntingdon (with whom Goodyer has been staying), sheds light on Donne's relations with patrons.

Sir,

At some later reading I was more affected with that part of your letter which is of the book and the nameless letters than at first. I am not sorry, for that affection were for a jealousy or suspicion of a flexibility in you. But I am angry that any should think you had in your religion peccant humours defective or abundant,[1] or that such a book (if I mistake it not) should be able to work upon you. My comfort is that their judgement is too weak to endanger you since by this it confesses that it mistakes you in thinking you irresolved or various [changeable]. Yet let me be bold to fear that that sound, true opinion that in all Christian professions there is way

---

1 Donne is mistaken about the author, who was in fact the moderate Flemish Catholic Georg Cassander.

---

1 It was traditionally believed that the maintenance of good physical and mental health depended on the extent to which the four fluids known as humours were balanced. Donne is angered by the thought of Goodyer's religious views being criticised as unhealthy.

to salvation (which I think you think) may have been so incommodiously or intempestively [unseasonably] sometimes uttered by you, or else your having friends equally near, you of all the impressions of religion may have testified such an indifferency as hath occasioned some to further such inclinations as they have mistaken to be in you. This I have feared because heretofore the inobedient Puritans and now the overobedient Papists attempt you. It hath hurt very many, not in their conscience nor ends but in their reputation and ways, that others have thought them fit to be wrought upon. As some bodies are as wholesomely nourished as ours with acorns and endure nakedness, both which would be dangerous to us if we for them should leave our former habits, though theirs were the primitive diet and custom, so are many souls well fed with such forms and dressings of religion as would distemper and misbecome us and make us corrupt towards God, if any human circumstance moved it, and in the opinion of men (though none).

You shall seldom see a coin upon which the stamp were removed, though to imprint it better, but it looks awry and squint, and so for the most part do minds which have received divers [different] impressions. I will not, nor need to you, compare the religions. The channels of God's mercies run through both fields, and they are sister teats of his graces, yet both diseased and infected, but not both alike. And I think that, as Copernicism in the mathematics hath carried each farther up from the stupid [inanimate] centre and yet not honoured it nor advantaged it because, for the necessity of appearances, it hath carried heaven so much higher from it, so the Roman profession seems to exhale and refine our wills from earthly drugs and lees more than the Reformed, and so seems to bring us nearer heaven. But then that carries heaven farther from us by making us pass so many courts and offices of saints in this life in all our petitions and lying in a painful prison in the next[2] during the pleasure not of him to whom we go and who must be our judge, but of them from whom we come, who know not our case. Sir, as I said last time, labour to keep your alacrity and dignity in an even temper, for in a dark sadness indifferent things seem abominable or necessary, being neither, as trees and sheep to melancholic nightwalkers have unproper shapes. And when you descend to satisfy all men in your own religion or to excuse others to all, you prostitute yourself and your understanding, though not a prey, yet a mark and a hope and a subject for every sophister in religion to work on.

---

2 That is, purgatory.

For the other part of your letter, spent in the praise of the Countess,[3] I am always very apt to believe it of her, and can never believe it so well and so reasonably as now, when it is averred by you. But for the expressing it to her in that sort as you seem to counsel, I have these two reasons to decline it: that that knowledge which she hath of me was in the beginning of a graver course than of a poet, into which (that I may also keep my dignity) I would not seem to relapse. The Spanish proverb informs me that he is a fool which cannot make one sonnet and he is mad which makes two. The other stronger reason is my integrity to the other Countess,[4] of whose worthiness, though I swallowed your opinion at first upon your words, yet I have had since an explicit faith and now a knowledge, and for her delight (since she descends to them) I had reserved not only all the verses which I should make but all the thoughts of women's worthiness. But because I hope she will not disdain that I should write well of her picture, I have obeyed you thus far as to write, but entreat you by your friendship that by this occasion of versifying I be not traduced nor esteemed light in that tribe and that house where I have lived.

If those reasons which moved you to bid me write be not constant in you still, or if you meant not that I should write verses, or if these verses be too bad, or too good, over or under her understanding and not fit, I pray, receive them as a companion and supplement of this letter to you, and as such a token as I use to send, which use because I wish rather they should serve (except you wish otherwise), I send no other. But after I have told you that here at a christening at Peckham you are remembered by divers [several] of ours and I commanded to tell you so, I kiss your hands and so seal to you my pure love, which I would not refuse to do by any labour or danger.

Your very true friend and servant,
J. Donne

---

3 Elizabeth, Countess of Huntingdon.
4 Lady Bedford.

45

Letter XXXI. *To Sir Henry Goodyer*   Spring/Summer 1609

This extremely valuable letter voices Donne's low opinion of the official defence of the King's own apology for the oath of allegiance, written in reply to attacks by Catholics. His disgust with the slipshod methods of its author, William Barlow, the Bishop of Lincoln, seems to have been what impelled him to write his own defence of the oath, Pseudo-Martyr. (He noticeably conceals his low estimate of the government apologist's competence in Letter XXXVII, in which he dedicates his work to the King.)

Sir,

To you that are not easily scandalised and in whom, I hope, neither my religion nor morality can suffer, I dare write my opinion of that book in whose bowels you left me. It hath refreshed and given new justice to my ordinary complaint that the divines of these times are become mere advocates, as though religion were a temporal inheritance. They plead for it with all sophistications and illusions and forgeries, and herein are they likest advocates that, though they be feed [paid] by the way with dignities and other recompenses, yet that for which they plead is none of theirs.

In the main point in question, I think truly there is a perplexity (as far as I see yet), and both sides may be in justice and innocence, and the wounds which they inflict upon the adverse part are all *se defendendo* [in self-defence]. For clearly our state cannot be safe without the oath since they profess that clergyman, though traitors, are no subjects, and that all the rest may be none tomorrow. And, as clearly, the supremacy which the Roman Church pretend were diminished if it were limited, and will as ill abide that, or disputation, as the prerogative of temporal kings who, being the only judges of their prerogative, why may not Roman bishops (so enlightened as they are presumed by them) be good witnesses of their own supremacy, which is now so much impugned?

But for this particular author, I looked for more prudence and humane wisdom in him in avoiding all miscitings or misinterpretings because at this time the watch is set and everybody's hammer is upon that anvil, and to dare offend in that kind now is for a thief to leave the covert and meet a strong hue and cry in the teeth, and yet truly this man is extremely obnoxious [reprehensible] in that kind for, though he have answered many things fully (as no book ever gave more advantage than that which he undertook), and abound in delicate applications and ornaments from the divine and profane authors, yet, being chiefly conversant about two points, he prevaricates in both.

46

For, for the matter, which is the first, he refers it entirely and namely to that which Dr Morton hath said therein before, and so leaves it roundly. And for the person, which is the second, upon whom he amasses as many opprobries [reproaches] as any other could deserve, he pronounceth that he will account any answer from his adversary slander, except he do (as he hath done) draw whatsoever he saith of him from authors of the same religion, and in print. And so he, having made use of all the quodlibetaries [debating-points], imputations against the other, cannot be obnoxious himself in that kind, and so hath provided safely.

It were no service to you to send you my notes upon the book because they are sandy and incoherent rags for my memory, not for your judgement, and to extend them to an easiness and perspicuity would make them a pamphlet, not a letter. I will therefore defer them till I see you, and in the meantime I will adventure to say to you, without inserting one unnecessary word, that the book is full of falsifications in words and in sense, and of falsehoods in matter of fact, and of inconsequent and unscholarlike arguings, and of relinquishing the King in many points of defence, and of contradiction of himself, and of dangerous and suspected doctrine in divinity, and of silly, ridiculous triflings and of extreme flatteries, and of neglecting better and more obvious answers and of letting slip some enormous advantages which the other gave and he spies not. I know (as I begun) I speak to you, who cannot be scandalised, and that neither measure religion (as it is now called) by unity, nor suspect unity for these interruptions.

Sir, not only a mathematic point, which is the most indivisible and unique thing which art can present, flows into every line which is derived from the centre, but our soul, which is but one, hath swallowed up a negative and feeling soul which was in the body before it came and exercises those faculties yet. And God himself, who only is one, seems to have been eternally delighted with a disunion of persons. They whose active function it is must endeavour this unity in religion, and we at our lay altars (which are our tables or bedside or stools, wheresoever we dare prostrate ourselves to God in prayer) must beg it of him. But we must take heed of making misconclusions upon the want of it. For whether the mayor and aldermen fall out (as with us and the Puritans – bishops against priests) or the commoners' voices differ who is mayor and who aldermen or what their jurisdiction (as with the Bishop of Rome, or whosoever), yet it is still one corporation.

Your very affectionate servant and lover,

J. Donne

Mitcham, Thursday late

Never leave the remembrance of my poor service unmentioned when you see the good Lady.[1]

Letter XXXII. *To the Countess of Bedford*   1609

The 'petition for verse' mentioned in the third sentence of this letter seems to be the letter itself. It is tempting (though fruitless) to speculate whether Donne's poem 'Twickenham Garden' might have been some kind of reply to the verses which Lady Bedford, a poet herself as well as a patron of poets, had apparently shown him in her garden at Twickenham.

Happiest and worthiest Lady,

I do not remember that ever I have seen a petition in verse. I would not, therefore, be singular, nor add these to your other papers. I have yet adventured so near as to make a petition for verse. It is for those your Ladyship did me the honour to see in Twickenham garden, except you repent your making and having mended your judgement by thinking worse, that is, better, because juster, of their subject. They must needs be an excellent exercise of your wit which speak so well of so ill. I humbly beg them of your Ladyship with two such promises as to any other of your compositions were threatenings: that I will not show them, and that I will not believe them, and nothing should be so used that comes from your brain or breast. If I should confess a fault in the boldness of asking them or make a fault by doing it in a longer letter, your Ladyship might use your style and old fashion of the court towards me and pay me with a pardon. Here, therefore, I humbly kiss your Ladyship's fair, learned hands and wish you good wishes and speedy grants.

Your Ladyship's servant,
J. Donne

---

1 Presumably Lady Bedford.

Letter XXXIII. *To Sir Henry Goodyer*   1609

It is worth comparing this letter, with its complaints about the 'barbarousness' and 'insipid dullness' of the country and longing for the excitements of life at court, with Letter II. (The differences are, of course, due to the painful change in Donne's circumstances.)

Sir,

It should be no interruption to your pleasures to hear me often say that I love you and that you are as much my meditations as myself. I often compare not you and me but the sphere in which your resolutions are and my wheel – both, I hope, concentric to God, for methinks the new astronomy is thus appliable well, that we which are a little earth should rather move towards God than that he which is fulfilling, and can come nowhither, should move towards us.

To your life full of variety, nothing is old, nor new to mine, and as to that life all stickings and hesitations seem stupid and stony, so to this all fluid slipperinesses and transitory migrations seem giddy and feathery. In that life one is ever in the porch or postern, going in or out, never within his house himself. It is a garment made of remnants, a life ravelled out into ends, a line discontinued and a number of small wretched points, useless because they concur [converge] not, a life built of past and future, not proposing any constant present; they have more pleasures than we, but not more pleasure; they joy oftener, we longer; and no man but of so much understanding as may deliver him from being a fool would change with a madman which had a better proportion of wit in his often *lucidis* [lucid moments].

You know they which dwell farthest from the sun, if in any convenient distance, have longer days, better appetites, better digestion, better growth and longer life, and all these advantages have their minds who are well removed from the scorchings and dazzlings and exhalings of the world's glory. But neither of our lives are in such extremes, for you, living at court without ambition, which would burn you, or envy, which would divest others, live in the sun, not in the fire, and I, which live in the country without stupefying, am not in darkness but in shadow, which is not no light but a pallid, waterish and diluted one. As all shadows are of one colour, if you respect the body from which they are cast (for our shadows upon clay will be dirty, and in a garden, green and flowery), so all retirings into a shadowy life are alike from all causes and alike subject to the barbarousness and insipid dullness of the country. Only the employments and that

49

upon which you cast and bestow your pleasure – business or books – gives it the tincture and beauty. But truly, wheresoever we are, if we can but tell ourselves truly what and where we would be, we may make any state and place such. For we are so composed that if abundance or glory scorch and melt us, we have an earthly cave, our bodies, to go into by consideration and cool ourselves. And if we be frozen and contracted with lower and dark fortunes, we have within us a torch, a soul, lighter and warmer than any without. We are therefore our own umbrellas and our own suns.

These, sir, are the salads and onions of Mitcham, sent to you with as wholesome affection as your other friends send melons and *quelques choses* from court and London. If I present you not as good diet as they, I would yet say grace to theirs and bid much good do it you. I send you with this a letter which I sent to the Countess.[1] It is not my use nor duty to do so, but for your having of it. There were but two contents, and I am sure you have mine and you are sure you have hers. I also writ to her Ladyship for the verses she showed in the garden,[2] which I did not only to extort them nor only to keep my promise of writing (for that I had done in the other letter, and perchance she hath forgotten the promise), nor only because I think my letters just good enough for a progress [journey], but because I would write apace to her whilst it is possible to express that which I yet know of her, for by this growth I see how soon she will be ineffable.

Letter XXXIV. *To Bridget White*   29 June 1610

Donne's stylish and extravagant compliments often had an ulterior motive – as here, where his description of Mrs White as a soul that has gone to heaven and his claim that by leaving London she has killed it are the preludes to an implied, though gallant, reprimand: he is impatient to know why she has not responded to six letters he has sent her. (Mrs White had spent the early part of 1610 in London.)

Madam,

I could make some guess whether souls that go to heaven retain any memory of us that stay behind if I knew whether you ever thought of us

---

1 Lady Bedford.
2 See Letter XXXII.

since you enjoyed your heaven, which is yourself, at home. Your going away hath made London a dead carcass. A term and a court do a little spice and embalm it and keep it from putrefaction, but the soul went away in you, and I think the only reason why the plague is somewhat slackened is because the place is dead already and nobody left worth the killing.

Wheresoever you are, there is London enough, and it is a diminishing of you to say so since you are more than the rest of the world. When you have a desire to work a miracle, you will return hither and raise the place from the dead and the dead that are in it, of which I am one, but that a hope that I have a room in your favour keeps me alive, which you shall abundantly confirm to me if by one letter you tell me that you have received my six. For now my letters are grown to that bulk that I may divide them, like Amadis the Gaul's book, and tell you that this is the first letter of the second part of the first book.

Your humblest and affectionate servant,
J.D.
Strand, St Peter's Day at nine

Letter XXXV. *To Bridget White*   29 June 1610

In the hours that elapsed between writing Letter XXXIV and this, Donne seems to have decided to try a more direct approach to the question of his unanswered letters.

Madam,

I think the letters which I send to you single lose themselves by the way for want of a guide, or faint for want of company. Now, that on your part there be no excuse, after three single letters I send three together that every one of them may have two witnesses of their delivery. They come also to wait upon another letter from Sir Edward Herbert, of whose recovery from a fever you may apprehend a perfecter contentment than we because you had none of the former sorrow. I am an heretic if it be sound doctrine that pleasure tastes best after sorrow. For my part, I can love health well enough though I be never sick, and I never needed my mistress's frowns and disfavours to make her favours acceptable to me. In states it is a weakness to stand upon a defensive war and safer not to be invaded than to have overcome. So in our souls' health, an innocency is better than the heartiest repentance, and in the pleasures of this life it is better that the variety of

the pleasures give us the taste and appetite to it than a sour and sad interruption quicken our stomach [appetite], for then we live by physic
[medicine]. I wish, therefore, all your happinesses such as this entire and
without flaw or spot of discontentment, and such is the love and service of

Your humblest and affectionate servant,

J.D.

Strand, St Peter's Day at four

Letter XXXVI. *To Bridget White*   Summer/Autumn 1610

This letter, which implies that Donne has still heard nothing from Mrs White, was
not sent until 8 November, having 'languished upon [his] table for a passage',
according to a note written to accompany it. We know, however,
that Donne was capable of viewing an unsent letter with great pleasure
(see Letter XXI).

Madam,

I have but small comfort in this letter. The messenger comes too easily
to me, and I am too sure that the letter shall be delivered. All adventures
towards you should be of more difficulty and hazard. But perchance I need
not lament this. It may be so many of my letters are lost already that it is
time that one should come, like Job's servant, to bring word that the rest
were lost. If you have had more before, this comes to ask how they were
received, and if you have had none, it comes to try how they should
[would] have been received. It comes to you like a bashful servant, who,
though he have an extreme desire to put himself in your presence, yet hath
not much to say when he is come. Yet hath it as much to say as you can
think, because what degrees soever of honour, respect and devotion you
can imagine or believe to be in any, this letter tells you that all those are
in me towards you, so that for this letter you are my secretary. For your
worthiness and your opinion that I have a just estimation of them, write
it, so that it is as long and as good as you think it, and nothing is left to me
but, as a witness, to subscribe the name of

Your most humble servant,

J.D.

Though this letter be yours, it will not misbecome or disproportion it that

52

I mention your noble brother, who is gone to Cleves not to return till towards Christmas, except the business deserve him not so long.

Letter XXXVII. *To King James I*   1610

Seventeenth-century letters of dedication shamelessly flattered their addressees, and Donne's letter dedicating his book Pseudo-Martyr *to James I is no exception. Ostensibly designed to persuade Catholics that it was compatible with their beliefs to swear the oath of allegiance, the book was a bid for royal favour: the best-known defence of the oath to date was the King's own, and a number of those who were eager for preferment decided that flattery by imitation was their best course.*

Most mighty and sacred Sovereign,

As temporal armies consist of pressed men and voluntaries, so do they also in this warfare in which your Majesty hath appeared by your books. And not only your strong and full garrisons, which are your clergy and your universities, but also obscure villages can minister soldiers. For the equal interest which all your subjects have in the cause, all being equally endangered in your dangers, gives every one of us a title to the dignity of this warfare, and so makes those whom the civil laws made opposite all one – *paganos, milites* [makes soldiers of peasants]. Besides, since in this battle your Majesty, by your books, is gone in person out of the kingdom, who can be exempt from waiting upon you in such an expedition? For this oath must work upon us all, and as it must draw from the papists a profession, so it must from us a confirmation of our obedience. They must testify an allegiance by the oath, we an allegiance to it. For since, in providing for your Majesty's security, the oath defends us, it is reason that we defend it. The strongest castle that is cannot defend the inhabitants if they sleep or neglect the defence of that which defends them. No more can this oath, though framed with all advantageous Christianly wisdom, secure your Majesty, and us in you, if by our negligence we should open it either to the adversary's batteries or to his underminings.

The influence of those your Majesty's books as the sun, which penetrates all corners, hath wrought upon me and drawn up and exhaled from my poor meditations these discourses, which, with all reverence and devotion, I present to your Majesty, who in this also have the power and office of the sun, that those things which you exhale you may at your pleasure dissipate and annul, or suffer them to fall down again as a wholesome and fruitful dew upon your Church and commonwealth. Of my boldness in this address I most humbly beseech your Majesty to admit this excuse, that having observed how much your Majesty had vouchsafed to descend to a conversation with your subjects by way of your books, I also conceived an ambition of ascending to your presence by the same way, and of participating by this means their happiness of whom that saying of the Queen of Sheba may be usurped: 'Happy are thy men and happy are those thy servants which stand before thee always and hear thy wisdom.'[1] For in this I make account that I have performed a duty by expressing, in an exterior and (by your Majesty's permission) a public act, the same desire which God hears in my daily prayers: that your Majesty may very long govern us in your person and ever in your race and progeny.

Your Majesty's most humble and loyal subject,
John Donne

Letter XXXVIII. *To Sir Henry Goodyer*   November 1611

By the time he wrote this letter, Donne's plans for accompanying a new patron, Sir Robert Drury, on a trip to France were well advanced. In an undated Latin letter to Goodyer, he mentions his unwillingness to leave behind his pregnant wife and seven children while he made a lengthy trip abroad, but he eventually arranged for them to stay with one of Ann's relatives on the Isle of Wight.

Sir,
I am near the execution of that purpose for France. Though I may have other ends, yet if it do but keep me awake, it recompenses me well. I am now in the afternoon of my life, and then it is unwholesome to sleep. It is ill to look back or give over in a course, but worse never to set out.

I speak to you at this time of departing as I should do at my last upon my deathbed, and I desire to deliver into your hands a heart and affections as innocent towards you as I shall to deliver my soul into God's hands then. I say not this out of diffidence, as though you doubted it, or that this should

---

1   1 Kings 10:8.

look like such an excuse as implied an accusation, but because my fortune hath burdened you so as I could not rectify it before my going, my conscience and interpretation (severer, I hope, than yours towards myself) calls that a kind of demerit, but God, who hath not only afforded us a way to be delivered from our great many debts contracted by our executorship to Adam but also another for our particular debts after, hath not left poor men unprovided for discharge of moral and civil debts, in which acknowledgement and thankfulness is the same as repentance and contrition is in spiritual debts. And though the value and dignity of all these be not perchance in the things but in the acceptation, yet I cannot doubt of it, either in God or you.

But, sir, because there is some degree of thankfulness in asking more (for that confesses all former obligations, and a desire to be still in the same dependency), I must entreat you to continue that wherein you have most expressed your love to me, which is to maintain me in the same room in my Lady Bedford's opinion in the which you placed me. I profess to you that I am too much bound to her for expressing every way her care of my fortune that I am weary before she is, and out of a loathness that so good works should be bestowed upon so ill stuff or that so much ill fortune should be mingled with hers as that she should miss anything that she desired, though it were but for me, I am willing to depart from farther exercising her endeavours in that kind. I shall be bold to deliver my poor letters to her Ladyship's hands through yours whilst I am abroad, though I shall ever account myself at home while I am in your memory.

Your affectionate servant and lover,
J. Donne

Letter XXXIX. *To George Garrard*   December 1611

This is the first letter Donne wrote to Garrard from France. It betrays his characteristic anxiety over whether it is destined to reach its addressee for, despite being a seasoned traveller, Donne does not seem to have discussed with Garrard, one of his two or three closest male friends, how best to contact him in his absence. Drury had arranged to rent a house in Amiens for his family and large entourage (including Donne).

Sir,

I would I were so good an alchemist to persuade you that all the virtue of the best affections that one could express in a sheet were in this rag of paper. It becomes my fortune to deal thus in single money, and I may hit better with this hail-shot of little letters (because they may come thick) than with great bullets, and trouble my friends less. I confess it were not long enough if it came to present my thanks for all the favours you have done me. But since it comes to beg more, perchance it may be long enough because I know not how short you will be with an absent friend.

If you will but write that you give me leave to keep that name still, it shall be the gold of your letter, and for allay [alloy], put in as much news as you will. We are in a place where scarce any money appears but base, as, I confess, all matters of letters is in respect of the testimonies of friendship. But obey the corruption of this place and fill your letters with worse stuff than your own.

Present my service to all those gentlemen whom I had the honour to serve at our lodging. I cannot fly an higher pitch than to say that I am so much their servant as you can say I am. At the Queen's Arms in Cheapside, which is a mercer's, you may hear of one Mr John Brewer, who will convey any letter directed to me at Sir Robert Drury's at Amiens, though he know not me, and I should be glad to hear that this first that I sent into England had the fortune to find you.

Yours,
J. Donne
Amiens

Letter XL. *To Sir Henry Goodyer*   January 1612

Here, in addition to voicing his famous complaint about the dullness of abroad, Donne rather surprisingly (in view of his general practice) defines letters worthy of the name as those which offer their recipients 'a convenient handsome body of news'. The letter then proceeds, unusually, to do precisely that, perhaps because its writer's boredom has forced him to take an interest in the comings and goings at the French court.

Sir,

That which is at first but a visitation and a civil office comes quickly to be a haunting and an uncivil importunity. My often writing might be subject to such a misinterpretation if it were not to you, who, as you know that the affection which suggests and dictates them is ever one and continual and uninterrupted, may be pleased to think my letters so too, and that all the pieces make but one long letter, and so I know you would not grudge to read any entire book of mine at that pace as you do my letters, which is a leaf a week, especially such letters as mine which (perchance out of the dullness of the place) are so empty of any relations as that they oppress not your meditations, nor discourse, nor memory.

You know that, for air, we are sure we apprehend and enjoy it, but when this air is rarefied into fire, we begin to dispute whether it be an element or no. So, when letters have a convenient handsome body of news, they are letters, but when they are spun out of nothing, they are nothing, or but apparitions and ghosts with such hollow sounds as he that hears them knows not what they said.

You (I think) and I am much of one sect in the philosophy of love, which, though it be directed upon the mind, doth inhere in the body and find plenty entertainment there. So have letters for their principal office to be seals and testimonies of mutual affection, but the materials and fuel of them should be a confident and mutual communicating of those things which we know.

How shall I then, who know nothing, write letters? Sir, I learn knowledge enough out of yours to me. I learn that there is truth and firmness and an earnestness of doing good alive in the world, and therefore, since there is so good company in it, I have not so much desire to go out of it as I had if my fortune would afford me any room in it. You know I have been no coward nor unindustrious in attempting that. Nor will I give it over yet. If at last I must confess that I died ten years ago, yet as the primitive Church admitted some of the Jews' ceremonies, not for perpetual use but because they would [wanted to] bury the synagogue honourably, though I died at a blow then when my courses were diverted, yet it will please me a little to have had a long funeral and to have kept myself so long above ground without putrefaction. But this is melancholic discourse.

To change, therefore, from this metaphorical death to the true, and that with a little more relish of mirth, let me tell you the good nature of the executioner of Paris, who, when Vatan was beheaded (who, dying in the profession of the religion, had made his peace with God in the prison, and so said nothing at the place of execution), swore he had rather execute forty Huguenots than one Catholic because the Huguenot used so few words and troubled him so little in respect of the dilatory ceremonies of the others in dying.

Cotton, the great court Jesuit, hath so importuned the Queen to give some modifications to the late interlocutory arrest against the Jesuits that in his presence the Count Soissons, who had been present in the court at the time of the arrest, and Servien, the King's advocate, who urged it, and the Premier President were sent for. They came so well provided with their books, out of which they assigned to the Queen so many so evident places of seditious doctrine that the Queen was well satisfied that it was fit by all means to provide against the teaching of the like doctrine in France.

The Duke of Epernon is come to Paris with (they say) 600 horse in his train, all which company came with him into the court, which is an insolency remarkable here. They say that scarce any of the princes appear in the streets but with very great trains. No one enemy could waste the treasures of France so much as so many friends do, for the Queen dares scarce deny any, that so she may have the better leave to make haste to advance her Marquis of Ancre, of whose greatness for matter of command or danger they have no great fear, he being no very capable nor stirring man, and then, for his drawing of great benefits from the Queen, they make use of it that their suits pass with less opposition. I believe the treasure is scattered because I see the future receipt charged with so very many and great pensions.

The Queen hath adventured a little to stop this rage of the princes' importunity by denying a late suit of Soissons, which though the other princes grudge not that Soissons should fail (for he hath drawn infinite sums already), yet they resent it somewhat tenderly that any of them should be denied when the Marquis obtains.

That which was most observed in the King's more childish age, when I was last here,[1] by those whom his father appointed to judge by an assiduous observation his natural inclination is more and more confirmed: that his inclinations are cruel and tyrannous. And when he is in any way affected, his stammering is so extreme as he can utter nothing. They cannot draw him to look upon a son of the Marquis whom they have put into his service, and he was so extremely affectionate towards the younger son of Beaufort that they have removed him to a charge which he hath, as he is made Prior of Malta. But yet there pass such letters between them by stealth

---

1 In 1605–6.

and practice as (though it be between children) it is become a matter of state and much diligence used to prevent the letters. For the young Marquis of Verneuil, the King speaks often of transplanting him into the Church, and once this Christmas delighted himself to see his young brother in a cardinal's habit.

Sir, it is time to take up [draw to an end], for I know that anything from this place, as soon as it is certain, is stale. I have been a great while more mannerly [deferential] towards my Lady Bedford than to trouble her with any of mine own verses but, having found these French verses accompanied with a great deal of reputation here, I could not forbear to ask her leave to send them. I writ to you by Mr Pory the 17 of January here and he carried that letter to Paris to gather news like a snowball. He told me that Pindar is gone to Constantinople with commission to remove and succeed Glover. I am afraid you have neglected that business. Continue me in Mr Martin's good opinion. I know I shall never fall from it by any demerit of mine, and I know I need not fear it out of any slackness or slipperiness in him, but much business may strangle me in him. When it shall not trouble you to write to me, I pray, do me the favour to tell me how many you have received from me, for I have now much just reason to imagine that some of my packets have had more honour than I wished them, which is to be delivered into the hands of greater personages than I addressed them unto.

Hold me still in your own love and proceed in that noble testimony of it of which your letter by Mr Pory spoke (which is the only letter that I have received since I came away), and believe me that I shall ever with much affection and much devotion join both your fortune and your last, best happiness with the desire of mine own in all my civil and divine wishes as the only retribution in the power of

Your affectionate servant,
Jo. Donne

Letter XLI. *Addressee unknown*   February 1612

It has been conjectured that this letter was written to Martha Garrard, George's sister. Certainly the letter Donne is known to have written to Martha Garrard from Spa (Letter XLV) and Letter L show that he was in the habit of addressing the kind of extravagant compliments to her which we tend to associate with his letters to patrons.

Madam,

I am not come out of England if I remain in the noblest part of it, your mind, yet I confess it is too much diminution to call your mind any part of England or of this world since every part even of your body deserves titles of higher dignity. No prince would be loath to die that were assured of so fair a tomb to preserve his memory. But I have a greater advantage than so, for since there is a religion in friendship and a death in absence to make up an entire frame, there must be a heaven too, and there can be no heaven so proportional to that religion and that death as your favour. And I am gladder that it is a heaven than that it were a court or any other high place of this world because I am likelier to have a room there than here, and better cheap.

Madam, my best treasure is time, and my best employment of that is to study good wishes for you, in which I am by continual meditation so learned that your own good angel, when it would do you most good, might be content to come and take instructions from

Your humble and affectionate servant,

J. Donne

Letter XLII. *To George Garrard*   February 1612

Donne is now as anxious about his lack of letters from home as about whether his own are getting through — further evidence of the truth of his large claims about the significance to him of the receipt, as well as the writing, of letters.

John Pory was in France to deliver a parcel of books by Lancelot Andrewes and the irenicist Isaac Casaubon from James I to Cardinal Perron. One imagines that Donne would have been interested in this instance of practical ecumenism (see Letters XXVI, XXIX and XXX).

Sir,

All your other letters, which came to me by more hazardous ways, had therefore much merit in them, but for your letter by Mr Pory, it was but a little degree of favour because the messenger was so obvious and so certain that you could not choose but write by him. But since he brought me as much letter as all the rest, I must accept that as well as the rest.

By this time, Mr Garrard, when you know in your conscience that you have sent no letter, you begin to look upon the superscription and doubt [suspect] that you have broken up some other body's letter, but whosesoever it were, it must speak the same language for I have heard from nobody.

Sir, if there be a proclamation in England against writing to me, yet since it is thereby become a matter of state, you might have told Mr Pory so. And you might have told him what became of Sir Thomas Lucy's letter in my first packet (for any letter to him makes any paper a packet and any piece of single money a medal), and what became of Lady Kingsmill's in my second, and of hers in my third, whom I will not name to you in hope that it is perished and you lost the honour of giving it.

Sir, mine own desire of being your servant hath sealed me a patent of that place during my life, and therefore it shall not be in the power of your forbidding (to which your stiff silence amounts) to make me leave being

Your very affectionate servant,

J. Donne

Letter XLIII. *To George Garrard*   14 April 1612

The two Anniversaries whose printing Donne bitterly regrets here in view of the odium it was bringing him had been written to commemorate Elizabeth Drury, who had died in December 1610 at the age of fourteen. The first poem seems to have been written shortly before the Drurys and Donne left for France, the second soon after they reached Amiens.

Despite his claim that he had never viewed the law as anything more than a pastime, Donne had apparently written to Thomas Morton to ask about the advisability of taking a law degree if he was going to practise as a lawyer.

Sir,

Neither your letters nor silence needs excuse. Your friendship is to me an abundant possession, though you remember me but twice in a year. He that could have two harvests in that time might justly value his land at a high rate, but, sir, as we do not only then thank our land when we gather the fruit but acknowledge that all the year she doth many motherly offices in preparing it, so is not friendship then only to be esteemed when she is delivered of a letter or any other real office but in her continual propenseness [proneness] and inclination to it.

This hath made me easy in pardoning my long silences and in promising myself your forgiveness for not answering your letter sooner. For my purpose of proceeding in the profession of the law so far as to a title, you may be pleased to correct that imagination wheresoever you find it. I ever thought the study of it my best entertainment and pastime, but I have no ambition nor design upon the style.

Of my *Anniversaries*, the fault that I acknowledge in myself is to have descended to print anything in verse, which, though it have excuse even in our times by men who profess and practise much gravity, yet I confess I wonder how I declined to it, and do not pardon myself. But for the other part of the imputation of having said too much, my defence is that my purpose was to say as well as I could, for since I never saw the gentlewoman, I cannot be understood to have bound myself to have spoken just truths. But I would not be thought to have gone about to praise her or any other in rhyme, except I took such a person as might be capable of all that I could say. If any of those ladies think that Mistress Drury was not so, let that lady make herself fit for all those praises in the book and they shall be hers.

Sir, this messenger makes so much haste that I cry you mercy for spending any time of this letter in other employment than thanking you for yours. I hope before Christmas to see England and kiss your hand, which shall ever (if it disdain not that office) hold all the keys of the liberty and affection and all the faculties of

Your most affectionate servant,

J.D.

Paris

Letter XLIV. *To Sir Henry Goodyer*   14 April 1612

This is the only extant letter from France to voice any desire to know the outcome of his wife's pregnancy, and readers could be forgiven for thinking that Donne was more concerned with what was being said at home about the publication of his Anniversaries, *an anxiety which quickly resurfaces. Like a number of other letters of Donne's, this relegates news to a postscript, but it is unusual in holding out the prospect of more to follow.*

Sir,

I writ to you once this week before, yet I write again, both because it seems a kind of resisting of grace[1] to omit any commodity of sending into England and because any packet from me into England should go not only without just freight but without ballast if it had not a letter to you.

In letters that I received from Sir Henry Wotton yesterday from Amiens, I had one of the 8 of March from you and with it one from Mrs Dauntsey of the 28 of January, which is a strange disproportion. But, sir, if our letters come not in due order and so make not a certain and concurrent chain, yet if they come as atoms, and so meet at last by any crooked and casual application, they make up and nourish bodies of friendship, and in that fashion, I mean one or other, first or last, I hope all the letters which have been addressed to us by one another are safely arrived, except perchance that packet by the cook be not, of which before this time you are clear, for I received (as I told you) a letter by Mr Nathaniel Rich and if you sent none by him, then it was that letter which the cook tells you he delivered to Mr Rich, which with all my criticisms I cannot reconcile because in your last letter I find mention of things formerly written which I have not found.

However, I am yet in the same perplexity which I mentioned before, which is that I have received no syllable, neither from herself nor by any other, how my wife hath passed her danger, nor do I know whether I be increased by a child or diminished by the loss of a wife.[2]

I hear from England of many censures of my book of Mistress Drury. If any of those censures do but pardon me my descent in printing anything in verse (which if they do, they are more charitable than myself, for I do not pardon myself but confess that I did it against my conscience, that is, against my own opinion that I should not have done so), I doubt not but they will soon give over that other part of that indictment, which is that I have said so much, for nobody can imagine that I, who never saw her, could have any other purpose in that than that when I had received so very good testimony of her worthiness and was gone down to print verses, it became me to say not what I was sure was just truth, but the best that I could conceive. For that had been a new weakness in me, to have praised anybody in printed verses that had not been capable of the best praise that I could give.

---

1 The Calvinist doctrine of the 'irresistibility of grace' was hotly debated at the time.
2 The child had been stillborn.

Presently after Easter we shall (I think) go to Frankfurt to be there at the election, where we shall meet Sir Henry Wotton and Sir Robert Rich, and after that we are determined to pass some time in the Palatinate. I go thither with a great deal of devotion, for methinks it is a new kind of piety that, as pilgrims went heretofore to places which had been holy and happy, so I go to a place now which shall be so, and more, by the presence of the worthiest princess of the world, if that marriage proceed.[3] I have no greater errand to the place than that, at my return into England, I may be the fitter to stand in her presence, and that after I have seen a rich and abundant country in his best seasons, I may see that sun which shall always keep it in that height.

Howsoever we stray, if you have leisure to write at any time, adventure by no other way than Mr Brewer at the Queen's Arms, a mercer in Cheapside. I shall omit no opportunity, of which I doubt not to find more than one before we go from Paris. Therefore, give me leave to end this, in which, if you did not find the remembrance of my humblest services to my Lady Bedford, your love and faith ought to try all the experiments of powders and dryings and waterings to discover some lines which appeared not, because it is impossible that a letter should come from me with such an ungrateful silence.

Your very true poor friend and servant and lover,

J. Donne

This day begins a history of which I doubt not but I shall write more to you before I leave this town. Monsieur de Rohan, a person for birth next heir to the kingdom of Navarre after the King's children (if the King of Spain were weary of it), and for alliance son-in-law to Duc de Sully, and for breeding, in the wars and estate the most remarkable man of the religion,[4] being Governor of St Jean d'Angély, one of the most important towns which they of the religion hold for their security, finding that some distastes between the lieutenant and the mayor of the town and him were dangerously fomented by great persons, stole from court, rode post to the town and removed these two persons. He sent his secretary and another dependent of his to give the Queen satisfaction, who is so far from receiving it that his messengers are committed to the Bastille, likely to be presently tortured, all his friends here commanded to their houses, and the Queen's

---

3 James I wished to marry his daughter Elizabeth to the Elector Palatine, Frederick V. (The marriage took place in 1613.)

4 That is, Roman Catholic.

companies of light horse sent already thitherward, and foot companies preparing, which troops being sent against a place so much concerning those of the religion to keep, and where they abound in number and strength, cannot choose but produce effects worthy your hearing in the next letter.

Letter XLV. *To Martha Garrard*   16 August 1612

The present letter – scarcely more than an elaborate acknowledgement of the arrival of one from his addressee – and another written at about the same time to Goodyer make it clear that Donne was now looking forward to returning to England. (The return journey must have been imminent, for he was back in London at the start of September prior to travelling to the Isle of Wight to see his family.)

Madam,

The dignity and the good fortune due to your letter hath preserved a packet so well that through France and Germany it is at last come to me at Spa. This good experience makes me in despite of contrary appearances hope that I shall find some messenger for this before I remove, though it be but two days. For even miracles are but little and slight things when anything which either concerns your worthiness is in consideration or my valuation of it. If I fail in this hope of a messenger, I shall not grudge to do myself this service of bringing it into England, that you may hear me say there that I have thus much profited by the honour of your conversation and contemplation that I am, as your virtues are, everywhere equal, and that that which I shall say then at London I thought and subscribed at Spa, which is that I will never be anything else than

Your very humble and affectionate servant,

J. Donne

JOHN DONNE SELECTED LETTERS

Letter XLVI. *To Viscount Rochester*   1613

This letter opens a new and not very edifying chapter in Donne's career. More desperate for settled employment than ever, he decided to try his luck with the new royal favourite, Rochester, at the time of the general scrambling for office following the death of Robert Cecil, the Lord Treasurer. Rochester sought to marry the Countess of Essex – and needed a secretary, Sir Thomas Overbury having been committed to the Tower for openly opposing Rochester's pursuit of Lady Essex and her pursuit of a divorce.

My Lord,

I may justly fear that your Lordship hath never heard of the name which lies at the bottom of this letter. Nor could I come to the boldness of presenting it now without another boldness, of putting his Lordship who now delivers it[1] to that office. Yet I have (or flatter myself to have) just excuses of this and just ground of that ambition. For, having obeyed at last, after much debatement within me, the inspirations (as I hope) of the Spirit of God and resolved to make my profession divinity, I make account that I do but tell your Lordship what God hath told me, which is that it is in this course, if in any, that my service may be of use to this Church and state.

Since, then, your Lordship's virtues have made you so near the head in the one and so religious a member of the other, I came to this courage of thrusting myself thus into your Lordship's presence, both in respect that I was an independent and disobliged man towards any other person in this state, and delivered over now (in my resolution) to be a houschold servant of God. I humbly beseech your Lordship that since these my purposes are likely to meet quickly a false and unprofitable dignity which is the envy of others, you will vouchsafe to undertake or prevent or disable that by affording then the true dignity of your just interpretations and favourable assistance, and to receive into your knowledge so much of the history, and into your protection so much of the endeavours, of your Lordship's most humble and devoted servant.

---

1 See headnote to Letter XLVII.

66

Letter XLVII. *To Lord Hay*   1613

This is a covering note sent by Donne to Hay with Letter XLVI asking him to pass the letter on to Rochester. In the final paragraph he alludes to his intention of being ordained, also mentioned in the letter to Rochester, but the latter seems to have dissuaded him from such a course of action – for the present, at least.

My Lord,

I have told your Lordship often that I have no virtue but modesty, and I begin to fear that I lose that in saying so often that I have it. At least, if I were full freighted with it before, I find that at this time I make a desperate shipwreck of it. Either the boldness of putting myself by this way of letter into my Lord of Rochester's presence or the boldness of begging from your Lordship the favour of presenting it would spend more of that virtue than I have. But since I can strongly hope out of the general testimonies of his Lordship's true nobleness that he will allow me this interpretation, that I reserved myself till now when a resolution of a new course of life and new profession makes me a little more worthy of his knowledge, and that as soon as I had delivered myself over to God, I deliver myself to him, I cannot doubt of your Lordship's pardon for my boldness in using your mediation.

I did it not, my Lord, without some disputation. But I thought it very unworthy to have sent a first letter to his Lordship by a servant of my own, and to have made it the business of any friend of mine who hath the honour of accesses to him. I thought myself tied by that to have communicated my purposes with him, that person, and so to have foreacquainted another with that which I desire his Lordship should first know. For I make account that it is in one instant that I tell his and your Lordship that I have brought all my distractions together, and find them in a resolution of making divinity my profession that I may try whether my poor studies, which have profited me nothing, may profit others in that course, in which also a fortune may either be better made or at least better missed than in any other. One good fruit of it will be that my prayers for your Lordship's happiness shall be in that station more effectual with God, and that therein I shall best show myself to be your Lordship's most humble and thankful servant.

Letter XLVIII. *To Viscount Rochester*   1613

*One of his more abjectly self-effacing letters, this is designed to remind its addressee
either of Donne's existence or of some project that Rochester had agreed to further
but which, Donne fears, may have been forgotten. The highly ingenious reason he
proposes for seeing it as easy for Rochester to take up the project again relates to a
doctrine – the resurrection of the body – which was a persistent source of fascination
for him.*

My most honourable good Lord,

After I was grown to be your Lordship's by all the titles that I could
think upon, it hath pleased your Lordship to make another title to me by
buying me. You may have many better bargains in your purchases but
never a better title than to me, nor anything which you may call yours
more absolutely and entirely. If, therefore, I appear before your Lordship
sometimes in these letters of thankfulness, it may be an excusable boldness
because they are part of your evidences by which you hold me. I know
there may be degrees of importunity even in thankfulness, but your
Lordship is got above the danger of suffering that from me or my letters,
both because my thankfulness cannot reach to the benefits already received
and because the favour of receiving my letters is a new benefit. And since
good divines have made this argument against deniers of the Resurrection,
that it is easier for God to recollect the principles and elements of our
bodies, howsoever they be scattered, than it was at first to create them of
nothing, I cannot doubt but that any distractions or diversions in the ways
of my hopes will be easier to your Lordship to reunite than it was to create
them, especially since you are already so near perfecting them that if it
agreed with your Lordship's purposes, I should never wish other station
than such as might make me still [always] and only

> Your Lordship's most humble and devoted servant,
> J. Donne

Letter IL. *To the Countess of Bedford* 1613

Donne's acceptance of Sir Robert Drury's patronage must have put some strain on his relationship with Lady Bedford. On learning of the sensation created by the publication of his Anniversaries *(mentioned in Letters XLIII and XLIV), he had begun a verse letter to her with a view to explaining his decision to praise Elizabeth Drury so fulsomely. The letter printed below shows that on his return he continued to address Lady Bedford in his familiar, gallant style.*

Madam,

Amongst many other dignities which this letter hath by being received and seen by you, it is not the least that it was prophesied of before it was born, for your brother told you in his letter that I had written. He did me much honour both in advancing my truth so far as to call a promise an act already done, and to provide me a means of doing him a service in this act, which is but doing right to myself. For by this performance of mine own word I have also justified that part of his letter which concerned me, and it had been a double guiltiness in me to have made him guilty towards you. It makes no difference that this came not the same day nor bears the same date as his, for though in inheritances and worldly possessions we consider the dates of evidences, yet in letters, by which we deliver over our affections and assurances of friendship and the best faculties of our souls, times and days cannot have interest nor be considerable because that which passes by them is eternal and out of the measure of time.

Because, therefore, it is the office of this letter to convey my best wishes and all the effects of a noble love unto you (which are the best fruits that so poor a soil as my poor soul is can produce), you may be pleased to allow the letter thus much of the soul's privilege as to exempt it from straitness [constraints] of hours or any measure of times, and so believe it came then. And, for my part, I shall make it so like my soul that, as that affection of which it is the messenger begun in me without my knowing when any more than I know when my soul began, so it shall continue as long as that.

Your most affectionate friend and servant,
J.D.

Letter L. *To Martha Garrard*   1613

*The period 1613–14 is generally held to have been a low point in Donne's life (he
and his family were seriously ill during much of it), but this letter to George Garrard's
sister written shortly after a visit which Garrard had paid the Donnes in their new
premises in a house off Drury Lane belonging to Sir Robert Drury shows that he
was capable of at least sounding like his old self.*

Madam,

   Though there be much merit in the favour your brother hath done me
in a visit, yet that which doth enrich and perfect it is that he brought you
with him, which he doth as well by letting me see how you do as by giving
me occasions and leave to talk with you by this letter. If you have any
servant which wishes you better than I, it must be because he is able to put
his wishes into a better frame and express them better and understand
proportion and greatness better than I. I am willing to confess my impotency, which is that I know no wish good enough for you. If any do, my
advantage is that I can exceed his by adding mine to it. You must not think
that I begin to think thus when you begin to hear it by a letter. As sometimes by the changing of the wind you begin to hear a trumpet which
sounded long before you heard it, so are these thoughts of you familiar and
ordinary in me, though they have seldom the help of this conveyance to
your knowledge. I am loath to leave, for as long as in any fashion I can
have your brother and you here, you make my house a kind of Dorney.[1]
But since I cannot stay [detain] you here, I will come thither to you, which
I do by wrapping up in this paper the heart of

                                                  Your most affectionate servant,
                                                                 J. Donne

---

1 Dorney, in Buckinghamshire, was the Garrard family home.

Letter LI. *To Sir Henry Goodyer*   19 January 1614

Donne had offered to write an epithalamion to mark the marriage of Rochester and Lady Essex, once she had secured her divorce – the disputed 'nullity' referred to in the first paragraph of this letter. The offer was accepted and the poem duly written and presented (as it happens, after the wedding). Donne's projected defence of the divorce was never written; it could hardly have brought him much credit in the long term.

Sir,

I receive this here that I begin this return, your letter by a servant of Sir G. Greseley, by whom also I hasten this despatch. This needed no enlargement since it hath the honour to convey one from Mr Garrard. But though by telling me it was a bold letter, I had leave to open it, and that I have a little itch to make some animadversions and criticisms upon it (as that there is a cypher [zero] too much in the sum of the King's debts and such like), yet since my eyes do easily fall back to their distemper, and that I am this night to sup at Sir Arthur Ingram's, I had rather forfeit their little strength at his supper than with writing such impertinences. The best spending them is upon the rest of your letter, to which, sir, I can only say in general that some appearances have been here of some treatise concerning this nullity which are said to proceed from Geneva but are believed to have been done within doors by encouragements of some whose names I will not commit to this letter.

My poor study having lain that way, it may prove possible that my weak assistance may be of use in this matter in a more serious fashion than an epithalamion. This made me therefore abstinent in that kind. Yet by my troth I think I shall not scape. I deprehend [detect] in myself more than an alacrity – a vehemency [great eagerness] to do service to that company, and so I may find reason to make rhyme.

If it be done, I see not how I can admit that circuit of sending them to you to be sent hither (that seems a kind of praying to saints, to whom God must tell first that such a man prays to them to pray to him), so that I lose the honour of that conveyance, but for recompense you shall scape the danger of approving it. My next letter shall say more of this. This shall end with delivering you the remembrance of my Lady Bartlett, who is present at the sealing hereof.

Your very true and affectionate servant,
J. Donne

– which name, when there is any empty corner in your discourse with that noble lady at Ashby,[1] I humbly beseech you to present to her as one more devoted to her service than perchance you will say.

Letter LII. *To Sir Henry Goodyer*   February 1614

Ordination now lay less than a year away, and there is some justification for seeing the poverty which Donne claims would have made funerals difficult as an important factor in helping him finally determine on entering the Church. In fact two children would shortly need to be buried.

Sir,

I gave no answer to the letter I received from you upon Tuesday, both because I had in it no other commandment by it but to deliver your letter therein, which I did, and because that letter found me under very much sadness, which (according to the proportion of ills that fall upon me) is since also increased, so that I had not written now if I had been sure to have been better able to write next week, which I have not much appearance of. Yet there was committed to my disposition (that is, left at my house in my absence) a letter from Sir William Lower, but it was some hours after all possibility of sending it by the carrier, so that Mr W. Stanhope, giving me the honour of a visit at that time and being instantly to depart for your parts, did me the favour to undertake the delivery of it to you.

With me, sir, it is thus: there is not one person (besides myself) in my house well. I have already lost half a child, and with that mischance of hers, my wife fallen into an indisposition which would afflict her much but that the sickness of her children stupefies her, of one of which, in good faith, I have not much hope. This meets a fortune so ill-provided for physic and such relief that, if God should ease us with burials, I know not well how to perform even that. I flatter myself in this, that I am dying too. Nor can I truly die faster by any waste than by loss of children.

But, sir, I will mingle no more of my sadness to you, but will a little recompense it by telling you that my Lord Harrington, of whom a few

---

1 Lady Huntingdon.

days since they were doubtful, is so well recovered that now they know all his disease to be the pox and measles mingled. This I heard yesterday, for I have not been there yet. I came as near importunity as I could for an answer from Essex House, but this was all, that he should see you shortly himself.

Your servant,
J. Donne

I cannot tell you so much as you tell me of anything from my Lord of Somerset since the epithalamion,[1] for I heard nothing.

Letter LIII. *To the Earl of Somerset* March 1614?

Donne had no qualms about asking an influential patron to do what he could to secure a specific appointment for him: in 1608 it was a secretaryship in Ireland (see Letters XXVII and XXVIII), in 1614 the post of ambassador to Venice. It is perhaps as well that Donne's candidature was not forwarded: had he been a serious contender, he would have been in direct competition with a number of close friends such as Wotton and Drury.

My most honoured Lord,
    Since your Lordship will not let me die but have, by your favour of sending to me, so much prevailed against a vehement fever that I am now in good degrees of convalescence, I was desirous that my first sacrifice to any person in this world for my beginning of health should be to your Lordship, that I might acknowledge that, as ever since I had the happiness to be in your Lordship's sight, I have lived upon your bread, so I owe unto your Lordship now all the means of my recovery, and my health itself. So must all the rest of my life and means be a debt to your Lordship, from whom since I received a commandment so much to assist myself as to present to your Lordship whatsoever to appear to me likely to advantage me and ease your Lordship.
    I am now bold in obedience of that commandment to tell your Lordship that that is told me, that Sir Dudley Carleton is likely to be removed from

---

1 See headnote to Letter LI.

Venice to the States.[1] If your Lordship have no particular determination upon that place nor upon me, I humbly beseech your Lordship to pardon me the boldness of asking you whether I may not be sent thither. All the substance and all the circumstances of this I most humbly submit to your Lordship with a protestation as true as if I had made it six days since, when I thought myself very near an end, that I had rather be anything which arises out of your Lordship than any proposition of mine, and that I have been in possession of my farthest ambitions ever since I had the dignity of being your most, etc.

Letter LIV. *To Sir Robert Ker*   21 March 1614

For the context of this letter, see Letter LIII.

Sir,

I sought you yesterday with a purpose of accomplishing my health by the honour of kissing your hands. But I find by my going abroad that, as the first Christians were forced to admit some Jewish ceremonies only to bury the synagogue with honour, so my fever will have so much reverence and respect as that I must keep sometimes at home. I must, therefore, be bold to put you to the pain of considering me.

If, therefore, my Lord upon your delivery of my last letter said nothing to you of the purpose thereof, let me tell you now that it was that in obedience of his commandment to acquaint him with anything which might advantage me, I was bold to present that which I heard, which was that Sir Dudley Carleton was likely to be removed from Venice to the States, of which if my Lord said nothing to you, I beseech you, add thus much to your many other favours, to entreat my Lord at his best commodity to afford me the favour of speaking with him.

But if he have already opened himself so far to you as that you may take knowledge thereof to him, then you may ease him of that trouble of giving me an audience by troubling yourself thus much more as to tell him in my behalf and from me that though Sir Dudley Carleton be not removed, yet

---

1 That is, the Low Countries; this part of the letter was amended as printed here by Gosse: the text is manifestly corrupt at this point.

that place with the States lying open, there is a fair field of exercising his favour towards me and of constituting a fortune to me and (that which is more) of a means for me to do him particular services. And, sir, as I do thoroughly submit the end and effect of all projects to his Lordship's will, so do I this beginning thereof to your advice and counsel if you think me capable of it as for your own sake I beseech you to do, since you have admitted me for

Your humble servant,
J. Donne

Letter LV. *To Sir Robert Ker*   May 1614

This melancholy letter inspired by the death of Donne's three-year-old daughter Mary gains added poignancy when read in the light of Letter LII. Donne calls this a letter without a subject, a curious judgement in view of the much greater emptiness (from the point of view of information) of a number of other letters unless we take it as evidence that for Donne 'subject' meant 'debating-point'.

Sir,
    Perchance others may have told you that I am relapsed into my fever. But that which I must entreat you to condole with me is that I am relapsed into good degrees of health. Your cause of sorrow for that is that you are likely to be the more troubled with such an impertinency as I am, and mine is that I am fallen from fair hopes of ending all. Yet I have scaped no better cheap than that I have paid death one of my children for my ransom. Because I loved it well, I make account that I dignify the memory of it by mentioning it to you, else I should not be so homely. Impute this brevity of writing to you upon no subject to my sickness, in which men use to talk idly, but my profession of desiring to be retained in your memory impute to your own virtues, which have wrought so much upon

Your humble servant,
John Donne

Letter LVI. *To Sir Robert More*   10 August 1614

Comparatively little is known of Donne's relations with the Mores once they had accepted the fact of their daughter's marriage (see Letters V to X). However, this letter to his brother-in-law containing a rare tribute to his affection for Ann suggests that Donne was on good terms with her family – certainly good enough for him to feel able, in his straitened circumstances, to ask to borrow a horse.

Sir,

Since I had no other thing in contemplation when I purposed this journey than my health, methinks it is a kind of physic [medicine] to be so long about that, and I grow weary of physic quickly. I have therefore put off that purpose, at least till the King come into these parts. If your horse (which I return by this carrier of Guildford) have not found as good salads in our Covent Garden as he should at Loseley, yet I believe he hath had more ease than he should have had there. We are condemned to this desert of London for all this summer, for it is company, not houses, which distinguishes between cities and deserts. When I began to apprehend that even to myself, who can relieve myself upon books, solitariness was a little burdensome, I believed it would be so much more so to my wife if she were left alone. So much company, therefore, as I am, she shall not want, and we had not one another at so cheap a rate as that we should ever be so weary of one another.

Sir, when these places afford anything worth your knowledge, I shall be your referendary [reporter]. Now my errand is only to deliver my thanks and services, accompanied with your poor sister's, to yourself and all your good company.

Yours ever to be commanded,
J. Donne

I pray, sir, give this note enclosed to my Lady your mother. It is of some parcels which she commanded my wife to buy for her, which are sent down at this time by the carrier.

Letter LVII. *To Sir Henry Goodyer*   18 December 1614

Ever interested in the careers of those who might be able to forward his, Donne was at this time closely watching the rise of the latest royal favourite, George Villiers. It is not known whether Donne realised that Villiers had been introduced into the court by, among others, the Countess of Bedford, with a view to undermining the influence of Somerset: Donne certainly knew of Lady Bedford's hostility to Somerset, which had put him in a difficult position at a time when he was looking to Somerset for assistance.

Sir,

Since I received a letter by your son, whom I have not yet had the honour to see, I had a letter packet from you by Mr Roe. To the former I writ before. In this I have no other commandment from you but to tell you whether Mr Villiers have received from the King any additions of honour or profit. Without doubt he hath yet none. He is here, practising for the masque,[1] of which, if I misremember not, I writ as much as you desire to know in a letter which seems not to have been come to you when you writ. In the Savoy business the King hath declared himself by an engagement to assist him with £100,000 a year if the war continue, but I believe he must farm out your Warwickshire benevolence for the payment thereof. Upon the strength of this engagement Sir Robert Rich becomes confident in his hopes. If you stood in an equal disposition for the west and only forbore by reason of Mr Martin's silence, I wonder, for I think I told you that he was gone, and I saw in Sir Thomas Lucy's hand a letter from him to you which was likely to tell you as much. Since I came from court, I have stirred very little. Now that the court comes again to us, I may have something which you may be content to receive from

Your very affectionate,

J. Donne

---

1 Probably one of Ben Jonson's, which were frequently acted at court.

Letter LVIII. *To the Countess of Bedford*   Late 1614

The Countess of Bedford's younger brother John died of smallpox in February 1614 at the age of twenty-two. Donne knew him well, was genuinely affected by his early death, and eventually – under cover of this note – sent Lady Bedford an elegy he had written to commemorate him. His insistence that he does not expect anything in return suggests that his motives in writing it were not entirely altruistic.

Madam,

I have learned by those laws wherein I am a little conversant that he which bestows any cost upon the dead obliges him which is dead, but not the heir. I do not therefore send this paper to your Ladyship that you should thank me for it or think that I thank you in it. Your favours and benefits to me are so much above my merits that they are even above my gratitude if that were to be judged by words, which must express it.

But, madam, since your noble brother's fortune being yours, the evidences concerning it are yours, so, his virtue being yours, the evidences concerning it belong also to you, of which, by your acceptance, this may be one piece, in which quality I humbly present it, and as a testimony how entirely your family possesseth

Your Ladyship's most humble and thankful servant,

John Donne

Letter LIX. *To Sir Henry Goodyer*   20 December 1614

Written shortly before Donne's ordination, this letter shows him attempting to tie up some loose ends. He has been trying in particular to gather in his poems in order to publish them – a surprising development in view of the regrets over 'descending' to print his Anniversaries expressed in Letters XLIII and XLIV. The scheme came to nothing, no doubt partly because of the difficulty of getting hold of the poems. He would also have run the risk of irrevocably offending the Countess of Bedford by dedicating his collected poems to Somerset.

Sir,

I writ to you yesterday, taking the boldness to put a letter into the good

Lady's¹ packet for you. This morning I had this new occasion of writing, that Sir Thomas Roe, who brought this enclosed letter to me, and left it unsealed, entreated me to take the first opportunity of sending it. Besides that which is in that letter (for he read it to me), I came to the knowledge in York House that my Lord Chancellor² hath been moved [influenced] and incensed against you, and asking Sir Thomas Roe if he were directly or occasionally any cause of that, he tells me thus much, that Sir William Lower and Sir Henry Carey have obtained of my Lord to have a pursuivant and consequently a sergeant sent into the country for you. My Lord grounds this earnestness against you upon some refusing to appear upon process which hath been taken out against you, and I perceive Sir Edward Easton and both the others admit consultations of ways by petition to the King or Council or Lord Chamberlain³ or any other. The great danger obliquely likely to fall is that when it comes to light how you stand towards Mr Mathew, you may lose the ease which you have by colour of that extent, and he may lose the benefit of having had so much of his estate concealed. You will therefore at least pardon my advising you to place those sums which by your retiring I presume you do employ upon payment of debts in such places as that these particular friends be not forced to leave being so. I confess, the going about to pay debts hastens importunity. I find in myself that where I was not asked money before, yet when I offered to pay next term, they seem loath to afford me that time which might justly have been desperate before. But that which you told me out of the country, with the assistance which I hope to find here (especially if your endeavour may advance it at Dorset House),⁴ I hope will enable me to escape clamour and an ill conscience in that behalf.

One thing more I must tell you, but so softly I am loath to hear myself – and so softly that, if that good Lady were in the room with you and this letter, she might not hear. It is that I am brought to a necessity of printing my poems and addressing them to my Lord Chamberlain. This I mean to do forthwith, not for much public view but at mine own cost, a few copies. I apprehend some incongruities in the resolution, and I know what I shall suffer from many interpretations, but I am at an end of much considering that. And if I were as startling in that kind as ever I was, yet in this particular I am under an unescapable necessity, as I shall let you perceive when

---

1 Lady Bedford's.
2 Sir Thomas Egerton, now Lord Ellesmere.
3 Somerset.
4 Donne had been hoping for financial assistance from the Earl of Dorset.

I see you. By this occasion I am made a rhapsoder of mine own rags, and that cost me more diligence to seek them than it did to make them. This made me ask to borrow that old book of you, which it will be too late to see for that use when I see you, for I must do this as a valediction to the world before I take orders.

But this is it I am to ask you: whether you ever made any such use of the letter in verse *a notre comtesse chez vous* as that I may not put it in amongst the rest to persons of that rank,[5] for I desire very much that something should bear her name in the book, and I would be just to my written words to my Lord Harrington to write nothing after that.[6] I pray, tell me as soon as you can if I be at liberty to insert that, for if you have by any occasion applied any pieces of it, I see not that it will be discerned when it appears in the whole piece. Though this be a little matter, I would be sorry not to have an account of it within as little after New Year's tide as you could.

I have something else to say of Mr Villiers, but because I hope to see you here shortly, and because new additions to the truths or rumours which concern him are likely to be made by occasion of this masque, I forbear to send you the edition of this mart [details of this stage of the trading] since I know it will be augmented by the next, of which, if you prevent [forestall] it not by coming, you shall have by letter an account from

Your very affectionate friend and servant,
J. Donne

Letter LX. *To the Earl of Somerset*   1614?

The end of the first sentence of this letter shows why Somerset was in a position to be so useful to Donne – or so Donne had once believed. Otherwise the letter seems to be an attempt on Donne's part to remind Somerset of his existence, so little having so far come of a relationship from which Donne had hoped for so much.

---

5 Goodyer regularly plundered Donne's poems for phrases to use in his own.
6 In his poem commemorating the Countess's brother John, the second Lord Harrington (see Letter LVIII), Donne claimed to be renouncing poetry: his Muse had, he said, 'spoke her last'. What he writes here suggests that he saw his decision as binding. (Only a small number of Donne's extant poems date from after his ordination.)

It is now somewhat more than a year since I took the boldness to make my purpose of professing divinity known to your Lordship, as to a person whom God had made so great an instrument of his providence in this kingdom as that nothing in it should be done without your knowledge. Your Lordship exercised upon me then many of your virtues for, besides that by your bounty I have lived ever since, it hath been through your Lordship's advice and inspiration of new hopes into me that I have lived cheerfully. By this time, perchance, your Lordship may have discerned that the malignity of my ill fortune may infect your good, and that by some impressions in your Lordship I may be incapable of the favours which your Lordship had purposed to me. I had rather perish than be such a rub [impediment] in your fortune, or that through me your history should have one example of having missed what you desired.

I humbly therefore beg of your Lordship that, after you shall have been pleased to admit into your memory that I am now a year older, broken with some sickness and in the same degrees of honesty as I was, your Lordship will afford me one commandment and bid me either hope for this business in your Lordship's hand, or else pursue my first purpose, or abandon all. For as I cannot live without your favour, so I cannot die without your leave, because even by dying I should steal from you one who is by his own devotions and your purchase your Lordship's most humble and thankful servant.

Letter LXI. *Addressee unknown (Sir Henry Goodyer?)*   1614?

It has been conjectured that the following letter dates from 1625–7, but this would not make sense of Donne's remark about still being afflicted by what he calls 'this 'intemperance of scribbling'. It seems far more likely that this is a reference to the writing of his Essays in Divinity, *composed during the period before his ordination. Also in favour of this dating is the fact that Donne has been giving his 'meditations' the form of a sermon, and in* Essays in Divinity *he refers to what he has been writing as 'meditations' which 'lack thus much of sermons, that they have no auditory'.*

Sir,

I can scarce do any more this week than send you word why I writ not last. I had then seposed [set aside] a few days for my preparation to the communion of our Blessed Saviour's body, and in that solitariness and arraignment of myself digested some meditations of mine, and apparelled them (as I use) in the form of a sermon, for since I have not yet utterly delivered myself from this intemperance of scribbling (though I thank God my accesses are less and less vehement), I make account that to spend all my little stock of knowledge upon matter of delight were the same error as to spend a fortune upon masks and banqueting houses. I choose rather to build in this poor fashion some spittles [shelters for the sick] and hospitals where the poor and impotent sinner may find some relief, or at least understanding of his infirmity. And if they be too weak to serve posterity, yet for the present, by contemplation of them, etc.

Letter LXII. *To Sir Edward Herbert*   23 January 1615

Donne received ordination at the comparatively late age of forty-two from the Bishop of London, John King, who had been chaplain to Egerton at the time that Donne had been the Lord Keeper's secretary. In this letter he attempts to express his sense of being both changed and unchanged by the process of ordination. To mark the start of this new phase in his life, he had had a new seal, representing a cross and anchor, made for himself, and this is the earliest extant letter to have been stamped with it.

Sir,
      Because since I had the honour to see you or hear from you, I have received such a change as, if my unworthiness did not avile [dishonour] it, were an addition, I am bold to present to you the knowledge thereof, because thereby your power and jurisdiction, which is entirely over me, is somewhat enlarged. For as, if I should put any other stamp upon a piece of your gold, the gold were not the less yours, so (if there be not too much taken by me in that comparison) by having, by the orders of our Church, received a new character, I am not departed from your title and possession of me. But, as I was ever by my devotion and your acceptance your humble servant, so I am become by this additon capable of the dignity of being

Your very humble chaplain,
J. Donne
23 January 1615,
which was the very day wherein I took orders

Letter LXIII. *To Sir Henry Goodyer*   March 1615?

It was always frustrating for Donne when acquaintances retained a 'better memory' of his past life than he would have wished, and Lady Bedford's disapproval of his decision to become a clergyman seems to have caused her to be less generous with funds than he had hoped and she had promised (or so he believed). Donne's suspicions of Dr John Burgess, a former Puritan preacher, were probably well founded: Burgess had reinvented himself as a physician and ministered to Lady Bedford in both a medical and a spiritual capacity; he would hardly have approved of Donne.

Sir,

I had destined all this Tuesday for the court because it is both a sermon day and the first day of the King's being there. Before I was to go forth, I had made up this enclosed packet for you, and then came this messenger with your packet, of which, if you can remember the number, you cannot expect any account thereof from me, who have not half an hour left me before I go forth, and your messenger speaks of a necessity of returning homeward before my returning home. If upon the delivery of them, or any other occasion, there intervene new subject of writing, I shall relieve myself upon Tuesday if Tamworth carrier be in town.

To the particulars of the letter to myself I will give this paper and line. Of my Lady Bedford I must say so much as must importune you to burn the letter, for I would say nothing of her upon record that should not testify my thankfulness for all her graces. But upon this motion, which I made to her by letter and by Sir Thomas Roe's assistance, if any scruple should arise in her, she was somewhat more startling than I looked for from her. She had more suspicion of my calling, a better memory of my past life than I had thought her nobility could have admitted, of all which, though I humbly thank God I can make good use as one that needs as many remembrances in that kind as not only friends but enemies can present, yet I am afraid they proceed in her rather from some ill impression taken from Dr Burgess than that they grow in herself. But whosoever be the conduit, the water is the Holy Ghost's, and in that acceptation [sense] I take it.

For her other way of expressing her favour to me, I must say, it is not with that cheerfulness as heretofore she hath delivered herself toward me. I am almost sorry that an elegy[1] should have been able to move her to so much compassion heretofore as to offer to pay my debts, and my greater

---

1 See Letter LVIII.

wants now, and for so good a purpose as to come disengaged into that profession,[2] being plainly laid open to her, should work no farther but that she sent me £30, which in good faith she excused with that which is in both parts true: that her present debts were burdensome, and that I could not doubt of her inclination upon all future emergent occasions to assist me. I confess to you her former fashion towards me had given a better confidence, and this diminution in her makes me see that I must use more friends than I thought I should have needed. I would you could burn this letter before you read it: at least do when you have read it. For I am afraid out of a contemplation of mine own unworthiness and fortune that the example of this lady should work upon the lady where you are,[3] for though goodness be originally in her and she do good for the deed's sake, yet perchance she may think it a little wisdom to make such measure of me as they who know no better do.

Of any new treaty of a match with Spain I hear nothing. The wars in the Low Countries, to judge by their present state, are very likely to go forward. No word of a parliament, and I myself have heard words of the King as directly against any such purpose as any can sound. I never heard word till in your letter of any stirs in Scotland. For that of the French King which you ask, it hath this ground, that in the Assembly there a proposition hath been made and well entertained, that the King should be declared to have full jurisdiction in France, and no other person to have any. It hath much of the model and frame of our oath of allegiance, but with some modification. It is true, it goes farther than that state hath drove in any public declarations, but not farther than their schools have drove often and constantly. The easiness that it hath found in passing thus far without opposition puts (perchance unnecessarily) in me a doubt that they are sure to choke it at the royal assent, and therefore oppose it not by the way to sweeten the conveyance of their other purposes. Sir, if I stay longer I shall lose the text at court. Therefore I kiss your hand and rest

Your very true servant,
J. Donne

We hear (but without second [confirmation] as yet) that Sir Richard Phillips' brother in France hath taken the habit of a Capuchin.

---

2 Of clergyman.
3 Lady Huntingdon.

Letter LXIV. *To Sir Robert Ker* 17 April 1615

Donne was far from free of the anti-feminist prejudices of his period, as we see from this brief invitation to Ker to act as godfather at the christening of his daughter Margaret. (The christening was not allowed to interfere with his preparations for preaching his earliest extant sermon, delivered a few days later at Greenwich.)

Sir,

I have often sinned towards you with a presumption of being pardoned, but now I do it without hope and without daring to entreat you to pardon the fault, in which there are thus many degrees of importunity that I must beg of you to christen a child, which is but a daughter, and in which you must be content to be associated with ladies of our own alliance, but good women, and all this upon Thursday next in the afternoon. Sir, I have so many and so indelible impressions of your favour to me as they might serve to spread over all my poor race. But since I see that I stand like a tree which once a year bears no fruit yet this mast of children, and so am sure that one year or other I should afflict you with this request, I had rather be presently under the obligations and the thankfulness towards you than meditate such a trouble to you against another year. I was desirous this paper might kiss your hands as soon as you came, that if any other diversions made this inconvenient to you, I might have an excuse of your favour by knowing so much from you, who in every act of yours make me more and more

Your humble and thankful servant,
J. Donne

Letter LXV. *To His Mother* 1616

Although born and raised a Catholic, Donne apostatised at some time in the 1590s. Even his earliest sermons after his ordination in 1615 voice hostility to his childhood faith, but the pervasive religious tone of this letter, in which he comforts his mother on the recent death of his sister Anne, highlights his absolute refusal to condemn the Catholicism to which she had clung in spite of everything.

Donne's father died when he was only three or four years old. Richard Rainsford was Elizabeth Donne's third husband (and, like her first and second, a Catholic).

My most dear mother,

When I consider so much of your life as can fall within my memory and observation, I find it to have been a sea under a continual tempest, where one wave hath ever overtaken another. Our most wise and blessed Saviour chooseth what way it pleaseth him to conduct those which he loves to his haven and eternal rest. The way which he has chosen for you is strait [narrow], stormy, obscure and full of sad apparitions of death and wants and sundry discomforts, and it hath pleased him that one discomfort should still [continually] succeed and touch another that he might leave you no leisure, by any pleasure or abundance, to stay or step out of that way or almost to take breath in that way by which he hath determined to bring you home, which is his glorious kingdom.

One of the most certain marks and assurances that all these are his works, and to that good end, is your inward feeling and apprehension of them and patience in them. As long as the Spirit of God distils and dews his cheerfulness upon your heart, as long as he instructs your understanding to interpret his mercies and judgements aright, so long your comfort must needs be as much greater than others' as your afflictions are greater than theirs. The happiness which God afforded your first young time, which was the love and care of my most dear and provident father, whose soul, I hope, hath long since enjoyed the sight of our blessed Saviour, and had compassion of all our miseries in this world, God removed from you quickly, and hath since taken from you all the comfort that that marriage produced. All those children (for whose maintenance his industry provided, and for whose education you were so carefully and so chargeably diligent) he hath now taken from you. All that worth which he left, God hath suffered to be gone from us all, so that God hath seemed to repent that he allowed any part of your life any earthly happiness that he might keep your soul in continual exercise and longing and assurance of coming immediately to him.

I hope therefore, my most dear mother, that your experience of the calamities of this life, your continual acquaintance with the visitations of the Holy Ghost (which gives better inward comforts than the world can outward discomforts), your wisdom to distinguish the value of this world from the next, and your religious fear of offending our merciful God by repining at anything which he doth will preserve you from any inordinate and dangerous sorrow for this loss of my most beloved sister. For my part, which am only left now to do the office of a child, though the poorness of my fortune and the greatness of my charge hath not suffered me to express my duty towards you as became me, yet I protest to you before

Almighty God and his angels and saints in heaven that I do and ever shall esteem myself to be as strongly bound to look to you and provide for your relief as for my own poor wife and children. For whatsoever I shall be able to do, I acknowledge to be a debt to you, from whom I had that education which must make my fortune. This I speak not as though I feared my father Rainsford's care of you or his means to provide for you, for he hath been with me, and as I perceive in him a loving and industrious care to give you contentment, so I see in his business a happy and considerable forwardness.

In the meantime, good mother, take heed that no sorrow nor dejection in your heart interrupt or disappoint God's purpose in you. His purpose is to remove out of your heart all such love of this world's happiness as might put him out of possession of it. He will have you entirely. And, as God is comfort enough, so he is inheritance enough. Join with God and make his visitations and afflictions, as he intended them, mercies and comforts, and for God's sake pardon those negligences which I have heretofore used towards you, and assist me with your blessing to me and all mine, and with your prayers to our blessed Saviour that thereby both my mind and fortune may be apt to do all my duties, especially those that belong to you. God, whose omnipotent strength can change the nature of anything by his raising-Spirit of comfort, make your poverty riches, your afflictions pleasure, and all the gall and wormwood of your life honey and manna to your taste, which he hath wrought, whensoever you are willing to have it so, which because I cannot doubt in you, I will forbear more lines at this time amd most humbly deliver myself over to your devotions and good opinion of me, which I desire no longer to live than I may have.

Letter LXVI. *To Sir Edward Herbert*   4 April 1619

This letter and the two following it were written shortly before Donne's departure for Germany as chaplain to a diplomatic mission led by Doncaster following the start of the Thirty Years' War. This letter and Letter LXVII relate specifically to Biathanatos, the potentially inflammatory treatise on suicide which Donne had written some ten years earlier. He refused to destroy the book but was unwilling for it to be published, especially now that he was in orders.

Sir,

I make accompt [account] that this book hath enough performed that which it undertook, both by argument and example. It shall therefore the less need to be itself another example of the doctrine. It shall not therefore kill itself, that is, not bury itself, for if it should do so, those reasons by which that act should be defended or excused were also lost with it. Since it is content to live, it cannot choose a wholesomer air than your library, where authors of all complexions are presented. If any of them grudge this book a room, and suspect it of new or dangerous doctrine, you, who know us all, can best moderate. To those reasons which I know your love to me will make in my favour and discharge, you may add this: that though this doctrine hath not been taught nor defended by writers, yet they, most of any sort of men in the world, have practised it.

Your very true and earnest friend and servant and lover,
J. Donne

Letter LXVII. *To Sir Robert Ker*   April 1619

Donne's insistence, in this letter entrusting the manuscript of Biathanatos *to Ker, that the work was a product of his early, unreformed self — 'Jack Donne' as opposed to 'Dr Donne' — constitutes the earliest extant statement of the highly challenge-able idea that his life fell into these two phases. (It was certainly a useful way of explaining away any writing that came to embarrass him.)*

Sir,

I had need do somewhat towards you above my promises. How weak are my performances when even my promises are defective? I cannot promise – no, not in mine own hopes – equally to your merit towards me. But besides the poems of which you took a promise, I send you another book to which there belongs this history. It was written by me many years since, and because it is upon a misinterpretable subject, I have always gone so near suppressing it as that it is only not burnt. No hand hath passed upon it to copy it, nor many eyes to read it. Only to some particular friends in both universities then, when I writ it, I did communicate it. And I remember I had this answer, that certainly there was a false thread in it, but not easily found. Keep it, I pray, with the same jealousy. Let any that your discretion admits to the sight of it know the date of it, and that it is a book written by Jack Donne, and not by Dr Donne. Reserve it for me if I live, and if I die, I only forbid it the press and the fire. Publish it not, but yet burn it not – and between those do what you will with it. Love me still thus far for your own sake, that when you withdraw your love from me, you will find so many unworthinesses in me as you grow ashamed of having had so long and so much such a thing as

Your poor servant in Christ Jesus,

J. Donne

Letter LXVIII. *To the Countess of Montgomery*   April 1619

This letter resembles Donne's 'Hymn to Christ, at the Author's Last Going into Germany' and a valedictory sermon to his flock at Lincoln's Inn in transmitting a fear of not returning from Germany alive (see Letter LXVI). Commentators have tended to attribute his state of mind to his wife's death in 1617.

Donne followed the general practice of his time in delivering his sermons from notes, only writing them out afterwards for publication or to give to friends who wanted copies. The sermon requested by Lady Montgomery had been preached at Whitehall two months previously.

Madam,

Of my ability to do your Ladyship service anything may be an emblem good enough, for as a word vanisheth, so doth any power in me to serve you. Things that are written are fitter testimonies because they remain and are permanent. In writing this sermon which your Ladyship was pleased to hear before, I confess I satisfy an ambition of mine own, but it is the ambition of obeying your commandment, not only an ambition of leaving my name in the memory or in the cabinet. And yet, since I am going out of the kingdom and perchance out of the world (when God shall have given my soul a place in heaven), it shall the less diminish your Ladyship if my poor name be found about you. I know what dead carcasses things written are in respect of things spoken. But in things of this kind, that soul that inanimates them receives debts from them. The Spirit of God that dictates them in the speaker or writer and is present in his tongue or hand meets himself again (as we meet ourselves in a glass) in the eyes and hearts of the hearers and readers, and that Spirit, which is ever the same to an equal devotion, makes a writing and a speaking equal means to edification.

In one circumstance my preaching and my writing this sermon is too equal: that that your Ladyship heard in a hoarse voice then, you read in a coarse hand now. But in thankfulness I shall lift up my hands as clean as my infirmities can keep them and a voice as clear as his Spirit shall be pleased to tune in my prayers in all places of the world, which shall either sustain or bury

Your Ladyship's humble servant in Christ Jesus,
J.D.

Letter LXIX. *To Sir Toby Mathew*   August 1619

In the early stages of Doncaster's embassy (see Letter LXVI), the exiled Toby Mathew, son of the Archbishop of York and high-profile convert to Catholicism, wrote to both Doncaster and Donne offering them his assistance. Having decided that no harm could come from politeness towards someone with whom he had been on friendly terms a decade previously, Donne replied to Mathew with this conciliatory letter which nevertheless showed that he had heard that Mathew had been in the habit of maligning him.

Sir,

At Ratisbon I had your letter from Brussels, and in it, you. For my former knowledge of your ingenuity and mine own conscience [consciousness] of having demerited in nothing toward you are assurances to me that your professions are in earnest. I dare put myself upon the testimony of very many very good companies in England where your person and your history have been the discourse that I have never forsaken your honour and reputation. And you may be pleased to make this some argument of my disposition toward you, that when I have been told that you have not been so careful of me abroad, I have not been easy in believing it, and when at some times the authority of the reporter hath brought me to a half-belief of it, I have found other excuses in your behalf than a mere disaffection to me, and now I am safely returned to my first station again not to believe it.

If it could be possible that any occasion of doing you a real service might be presented me, you should see that that tree which was rooted in love and always bore leaves ready to shadow and defend from others' malice would bear fruit also. You know we say in the schools that grace destroys not nature. We may say too that forms of religion destroy not morality nor civil offices. That which I add I am far from applying to you, but it is true that we are fallen into so slack and negligent times that I have been sometimes glad to hear that some of my friends have differed from me in religion. It is some degree of an union to be united in a serious meditation of God and to make any religion the rule of our actions. Our sweet and blessed Saviour bring us by his way to his end! And be you pleased to be assured that no man desires to renew or continue or increase a friendship with you more than, etc.

Letter LXX. *To the Marquis of Buckingham*   8 August 1621

Donne had been led to believe that on the death of the Bishop of London, the Bishop of Lincoln would move to London and the Dean of Westminster, John Williams, would become Bishop of Lincoln, leaving the deanery of Westminster for the Dean of Salisbury and that of Salisbury for Donne. Donne has discovered that although Williams is indeed to be made Bishop of Lincoln, he is to be allowed to remain Dean of Westminster, and he here directs his disappointment at the man who misled him by telling him that he would be moving to Salisbury but on whose favour he still has to depend.

May it please your Lordship,

Ever since I had your Lordship's letter, I have esteemed myself in possession of Salisbury, and more than Salisbury, of a place in your service, for I took Salisbury as a seal of it. I hear that my Lord Keeper finds reason to continue in Westminster, and I know that neither your Lordship nor he knows how narrow and penurious a fortune I wrestle with in this world. But I am far from depending upon the assistance of any but your Lordship as that I do not assist myself so far as with a wish that my Lord Keeper would have left a hole for so poor a worm as I am to have crept in at. All that I mean in using this boldness of putting myself into your Lordship's presence by this rag of paper is to tell your Lordship that I lie in a corner as a clod of clay, attending what kind of vessel it shall please you to make of

Your Lordship's humblest and thankfullest and devotedest servant,
J. Donne

Letter LXXI. *To the Marquis of Buckingham*   13 September 1621

Events moved fast and Donne was told by James early in September 1621 that he was to be Dean of St Paul's. He then proceeded to write to Buckingham to thank him for securing the post for him, believing (or choosing to be thought to believe) that Buckingham was responsible – which, indeed, he may well have been: in later years Bishop Williams would claim responsibility for Donne's elevation, but such things tended not to be the work of a single individual.

My most honoured Lord,
    I most humbly beseech your Lordship to afford this rag of paper a room amongst your evidences. It is your evidence not for a manor but for a man. As I am a priest, it is my sacrifice of prayer to God for your Lordship; and as I am a priest, made able to subsist and appear in God's service by your Lordship, it is a sacrifice of myself to you. I deliver this paper as my image, and I assist the power of any conjuror with this imprecation upon myself, that as he shall tear this paper, this picture of mine, so I may be torn in my fortune and in my fame if ever I have any corner in my heart dispossessed of a zeal to your Lordship's service. His Majesty hath given me a royal key into your chamber, leave to stand in your presence, and your Lordship hath already such a fortune as that you shall not need to be afraid of a suitor when I appear there, so that I protest to your Lordship, I know not what I want since I cannot suspect nor fear myself for ever doing or leaving undone anything by which I might forfeit that title of being always
                              Your Lordship's, etc.
                              J.D.

Letter LXXII. *To Sir Henry Goodyer*   4 October 1622?

Even after his appointment as Dean of St Paul's, Donne's financial situation continued to dog him for some time: the immediate increase in his income was not enough to prevent him from falling farther into debt. It is easy to see where the money went if, as Walton claimed, the first thing Donne did when he moved into his deanery at the end of 1621 was to restore and beautify the chapel.

Sir,

All our moralities are but our outworks: our Christianity is our citadel. A man who considers duty but the dignity of his being a man is not easily beat from his outworks, but from his Christianity never, and therefore I dare trust you, who contemplates them both. Every distemper of the body now is complicated with the spleen, and when we were young men, we scarce ever heard of the spleen. In our declinations [declining states] now every accident is accompanied with heavy clouds of melancholy, and in our youth we never admitted any. It is the spleen of the mind, and we are affected with vapours from thence, yet truly even this sadness that overtakes us and this yielding to the sadness is not so vehement a poison (though it be no physic [medicine] neither) as those false ways in which we sought our comforts in our looser days.

You are able to make rules to yourself, and our blessed Saviour continue to you an ability to keep within those rules. And this particular occasion of your present sadness must be helped by the rule for, for examples, you will scarce find any, scarce any that is not encumbered and distressed in his fortunes. I had locked myself, sealed and secured myself against the possibilities of falling into new debts and, in good faith, this year hath thrown me £400 lower than when I entered this house. I am a father as well as you, and of children (I humbly thank God) of as good dispositions, and in saying so, I make account that I have taken my comparison as high as I could go, for in good faith, I believe yours to be so. But as those my daughters (who are capable of such considerations) cannot but see my desire to accommodate them in this world, so I think they will not murmur if heaven must be their nunnery, and they associated to the blessed virgins there. I know they would be content to pass their lives in a prison rather than I should macerate [worry] myself for them, much more to suffer the mediocrity of my house and my means, though that cannot prefer [advance] them. Yours are such too, and it need not that patience, for your fortune doth not so far exercise their patience. But to leave all in God's hands, from whose hands nothing can be wrung by whining but by praying, nor by praying without the *Fiat voluntas tua* [Thy will be done].

Sir, you are used to my hand and, I think, have leisure to spend some time in picking out sense in rags, else I had written less and in longer time. Here is room for an Amen. The prayer [here the text is defective] so I am going to my bedside to make for all you and all yours with

Your true friend and servant in Christ Jesus,
J. Donne

Letter LXXIII. *To Sir Henry Goodyer*   18 October 1622

With this brave account of a recent disappointment, Donne offers valuable insights into the processes by which seventeenth-century parents attempted to find suitable husbands for their daughters. He also (as in Letter LXXII) demonstrates his continuing lack of financial security.

Sir,

I would have intermitted this week [let this week pass] without writing if I had not found the name of my Lady Huntingdon in your letter. The devotion which I owe and (in good faith) pay in my best prayers for her good in all kind awakens me to present my humble thanks for this: that her Ladyship retains my name in her memory. She never laid obligation upon any man readier to express his acknowledgement of them to any servant of her servants. I am bound to say much of this for your indemnity because, though I had a little preparation to her knowledge in the house where I served at first, yet I think she took her characters [detailed impressions] of me from you. And at what time soever she thought best of me in her life, I am better than that, for my goodness is my thankfulness and I am every day fuller of that than before to her Ladyship. I say nothing to you of foreign names in this letter because your son Sir Francis is here. For that which you write concerning your son, I only gave my man Martin in charge to use his interest in the keeper that your son should fall under no wants [needs] there, which it seems your son discharged, for I hear not of them. For other trifles, I bade my man let him have whatsoever he asked so as it might seem to come from him and not me, and laying that look upon it, it came to almost nothing.

Tell both your daughters a piece of a story of my Con which may accustom them to endure disappointments in this world. An honourable person (whose name I give you in a schedule [accompanying note] to burn lest this letter should be mislaid) had an intention to give her one of his sons and had told it me, and would have been content to accept what I, by my friends, could have begged for her. But he intended his son to my profession and had provided him already £300 a year of his own gift in Church livings, and hath estated £300 more of inheritance for their children, and now the youth (who yet knows nothing of his father's intention nor mine) flies from his resolutions for that calling, and importunes his father to let him travel. The girl knows not her loss for I never told her of it, but truly it is a great disappointment to me. More than these, sir, we

must all suffer in our way to heaven, where I hope you and all yours shall
meet.

Your poor friend and affectionate servant,

J. Donne

Letter LXXIV. *To Sir Thomas Roe*   1 December 1622

*In this letter to Roe, the ambassador in Constantinople, to be carried by his chap-
lain along with one from James Hay, now Earl of Carlisle, Donne speaks remarkably
freely of the disquiet provoked by the projected Spanish match and as freely as he
dares of the constraint he had felt under when preaching the official defence of the
King's* Directions for Preachers *the previous September, the first of his sermons
to be printed.*

If your Lordship's chaplain be as well shipped as my letter is shipped in
him, they come both well to your Lordship. Mine is but a vessel for another
weather, for now when I begin to write, I remember a commandment
which my Lord of Carlisle laid upon me to call for a letter from him upon
the first commodity of sending, and before this letter be sealed, I hope he
will return from court. If he do not, I may have leave to say something
both of that which he would and that which he would not have said in his
own letter. He would not have said that which I may, that he is the directest
man that ever I knew, but he would have said that he is as much directed
upon you as any for, in good faith, he apprehends everywhere any occasion of testifying well of your Lordship. To speak in that language which
you know to be mine, that is free enough (at least) from flattery, he provides
for his ease and his thrift in doing so. For, truly, I have met no case
anywhere where the delivering of a good opinion of you or a judgement
upon any of your actions costs any man anything or exercises him against
an opposition. Our blessed Saviour give you the comfort of it all your way
and the reward of it at last.

Many grains make up the bread that feeds us and many thorns make up
the crown that must glorify us, and one of those thorns is, for the most
part, the stinging calumny of others' tongues. This (for anything that
concerned the public) you had not in your last employment, though then
you had a domestic Satan, a viper, a tongue-stinger in your own house. In
this employment you have been every way delivered from it. I never heard

your private nor public actions calumniated, so you have the less thorns to make up that crown. But, sir, since that crown is made of thorns, be not without them. When you contemplate Christ Jesus crowned with thorns, remember that those thorns which you see stand out hurt him not. Those which wounded him were bent inward. Outward thorns of calumny and misrepresentation do us least harm. Innocency despises them, or friends and just examiners of the case blunt or break them. Find thorns within. A wounding sense of sin bring you the thorns, and Christ will make it a crown, or do you make it a crown where two ends meet and make a circle (consider yourself from one mother to another, from the womb to the grave), and Christ will make it a crown of glory. Add not you to my thorns by giving any ill interpretations of my silence or slackness in writing. You, who have so long accustomed to assist me with your good opinion and testimonies and benefits, will not easily do that. But if you have at any time declined towards it, I beseech you, let this have some weight towards re-rectifying you, that the assiduity of doing the Church of God that service which (in a poor measure) I am thought to be able to do possesses me and fills me.

You know, sir, that the astronomers of the world are not so much exercised about all the constellations and their motions formerly apprehended and believed as when there arises a new and irregular meteor. Many of these this treaty of the marriage of the Prince hath produced in our firmament, in our divinity, and many men, measuring public actions with private affections, have been scandalised, and have admitted suspicions of a tepidness in very high places. Some civil acts in favour of the papists have been with some precipitation over-dangerously misapplied too. It is true there is a major proposition, but the conclusion is too soon made if there be not a minor too. I know to be sorry for some things that are done (that is, sorry that our times are overtaken with a necessity to do them) proceeds of true zeal, but to conclude the world upon the first degree of ill is a distilling with too hot a fire. One of these occurrences gave the occasion to this sermon, which by commandment I preached, and which I send your Lordship. Some weeks after that I preached another at the same place,[1] upon the Gunpowder Day. Therein I was left more to mine own liberty, and therefore I would I could also send your Lordship a copy of that, but that one, which (also by commandment) I did write after the preaching, is as yet in his Majesty's hand, and I know not whether he will in it, as he

---

1 Paul's Cross, the outdoor pulpit close to the cathedral.

did in the other after his reading thereof, command it to be printed. And whilst it is in that suspense, I know your Lordship would call it indiscretion to send out any copy thereof. Neither truly am I able to commit that fault, for I have no copy.

A few days after that I preached, by invitation of the Virginian Company, to an honourable auditory, and they recompensed me with a new commandment in their service to print that, and that, I hope, comes with this, for with papers of that kind I am the apter to charge your chaplain. In the exercise of my ministry I have assisted in the time of sickness, and now attended at the funerals, the first night of my Lady Jacob and the next of Sir William Killigrew, against whom the Bishop of Exeter, my predecessor here, had commenced a suit in Chancery of (as he laid it in his bill) £3,000 in value. The case grew to a strange point. That which was laid to him was indirect dealing in the execution of a commission about the value of that land which was taken from the bishopric. His sickness made him unable to answer. Without it they could not proceed. There was proposed a way to appoint him a guardian *ad hoc*, but the defect being not in his understanding, some of the judges said that if the case were treason and he by the hand of God become unable to answer, he could not be proceeded against. Whilst they were in farther deliberation, the good man is dead, and the charge being personal, and of which no other man can give an account, I hope the whole business is dead too, though, if it be pursued, I do not discern that they are in any danger. I recommend myself to your Lordship's prayers, and I enwrap you with mine own soul in mine, and our blessed God enwrap in the righteousness of his son both you and

Your Lordship's humblest and thankfullest servant in Christ Jesus,

J. Donne

At my poor house at St Paul's, London

Letter LXXV. *To the Marquis of Buckingham*   March–May 1623

From March to September 1623 Buckingham was in Spain to assist Charles with his ultimately unsuccessful wooing of the Infanta. Donne shared the widespread disapproval at home of the Spanish match (see Letter LXXIV) and here warns Buckingham of the danger of being taken in. Far from being amusingly ironical, he is hoping to alert Buckingham without offending him by too direct an approach to the topic.

Most honoured Lord,

I can thus far make myself believe that I am where your Lordship is – in Spain – that in my poor library, where indeed I am, I can turn mine eye towards no shelf in any profession, from the mistress of my youth, poetry, to the wife of mine age, divinity, but that I meet more authors of that nation than of any other. Their authors in divinity, though they do not show us the best way to heaven, yet they think they do, and so, though they say not true, yet they do not lie, because they speak their conscience. And since in charity I believe so of them for their divinity, in civility I believe it too, for civil matters, that therein also they mean as they say – and by this time your Lordship knows what they say.

I take, therefore, this boldness to congratulate [welcome] thus with your Lordship the great honour which you receive in being so great an instrument of that work in which the peace of Christendom so much consists. How to use a sword when it is out, we know you know. Think you that commandment of our Saviour's to be directed upon you: 'put up the sword.' Study the ways of peace. The hardest authors in the world are kings, and your Lordship hath read over the hardest of them. Since you have passed from the text of the King of Kings, the book of God, by the commentary of the wisest king amongst men, the counsels of our sovereign, the knowledge of other states and other kings is downhill and obvious to your Lordship, and you find it in posting [travelling]. And for this blessed clearness in your Lordship almighty God receives every day not the prayers (their time is not when the thing is given already), but the thanks of

Your Lordship's humblest and devotedest and thankfullest servant in
Christ Jesus,
J. Donne
Paul's

Letter LXXVI. *To Sir Robert Ker*   March–September 1623

Ker was in Spain with Prince Charles and Buckingham (see Letter LXXV). Here, too, Donne warns somewhat cryptically of the unsuitability of a match between Charles and the Infanta: east and west may meet, but not north (England) and south (Spain). The language and imagery of the second paragraph are put to rather different use in the sermon on which Donne had recently been working, mentioned in the final paragraph,[1] and also in his 'Hymn to God my God, in my Sickness', almost certainly written during his illness later in the year.

Sir,

Your way into Spain was eastward, and that is the way to the land of perfumes and spices. Their way hither is westward, and that is the way to the land of gold and of mines. The wise men who sought Christ laid down both their perfumes and their gold at the feet of Christ, the Prince of Peace. If all confer all to his glory and to the peace of his Church, Amen. But now I consider in cosmography better, they and we differ not in east and west: we are much alike easterly. But yet, *Oriens nomen eius*, the east is one of Christ's names in one prophet, and *Filius Orientis est Lucifer*, the east is one of the Devil's names in another – and these two differ diametrically. And so in things belonging to the worship of God, I think we shall. Amen.

But the difference of our situation is in north and south, and you know that, though the labour of any ordinary artificer in that trade will bring east and west together (for if a flat map be but pasted upon a round globe, the farthest east and the farthest west meet, and are all one), yet all this brings not north and south a scruple of a degree the nearer. There are things in which we may, and in that wherein we should not, my hope is in God and in him in whom God doth so evidently work, we shall not meet. Amen. They have hotter days in Spain than we have here, but our days are longer, and yet we are hotter in our business here, and they longer about it there. God is sometimes called a giant running a race, and sometimes is so slow-paced as that a thousand years make but a day with God, and yet still the same God. He hath his purposes upon our noble and vehement affections and upon their wary and sober discretions, and will use both to his glory. Amen.

---

1 *The Sermons of John Donne*, ed. George R. Potter and Evelyn M. Simpson, 10 vols (1953–62), VI, p.59.

Sir, I took up this paper to write a letter, but my imaginations were full of a sermon before, for I write but a few hours before I am to preach, and so instead of a letter I send you a homily. Let it have thus much of a letter, that I am confident in your love and deliver myself over to your service, and thus much of a homily, that you and I shall accompany one another to the possession of heaven, in the same way wherein God put us at first. Amen.

Your very humble and very thankful servant in Christ, etc.

Letter LXXVII. *To Sir Robert Ker*   February 1624?

Towards the end of 1623 Donne succumbed to the epidemic of relapsing fever which was gripping parts of London. It was uncertain whether he would survive, and the King sent his own physician to minister to him. Preternaturally alert to every detail of his illness, Donne charted its course in Devotions Upon Emergent Occasions, *which began being printed even before its author had fully recovered. (It was to prove extremely popular.) Here he consults Ker about the propriety of dedicating the work to the Prince of Wales.*

Sir,

Though I have left my bed, I have not left my bedside. I sit there still and, as a prisoner discharged sits at the prison door to beg fees, so sit I here to gather crumbs. I have used this leisure to put the meditations had in my sickness into some such order as may minister some holy light. They arise to so many sheets (perchance twenty) as that, without staying for that furniture of an epistle,[1] that [as?] my friends importuned me to print them, I importune my friends to receive them printed. That being in hand, through this long trunk that reaches from St Paul's to St James's I whisper into your ear this question: whether there be any uncomeliness or unseasonableness in presenting matter of devotion or mortification to that Prince whom, I pray God, nothing may ever mortify but holiness. If you allow my purposes in general, I pray, cast your eye upon the title and the epistle, and rectify me in them. I submit substance and circumstance to you and the poor author of both.

Your very humble and very thankful servant in Christ Jesus,
J. Donne

---

1 A letter of dedication.

Letter LXXVIII. *To Lady Kingsmill*   26 October 1624

There are no extant letters from Donne to Lady Kingsmill (formerly Bridget White) from the period between the writing of Letters XXXIV to XXXVI and the present letter, which was inspired by the death of her husband, though a sentence in Letter XLII makes it clear that they had continued to correspond after Lady Kingsmill's marriage towards the end of 1610.
This is arguably the most conventional of Donne's letters of condolence.

Madam,

Those things which God dissolves at once, as he shall do the sun and moon and those bodies at the last conflagration, he never intends to reunite again. But in those things which he takes in pieces, as he does man and wife in these divorces by death and in single persons by the divorce of body and soul, God hath another purpose to make them up again. That piece which he takes to himself is presently cast in a mould and in an instant made fit for his use, for heaven is not a place of proficiency but of present perfection. That piece which he leaves behind in this world by the death of a part thereof grows fitter and fitter for him by the good use of his corrections and the entire conformity to his will.

Nothing disproportions us nor makes us so uncapable of being reunited to those whom we loved here as murmuring [complaining] or not advancing the goodness of him who hath removed them from hence. We would wonder to see a man who in a wood were left to his liberty to fell what trees he would take only the crooked and leave the straightest trees, but that man hath perchance a ship to build and not a house, and so hath use of that kind of timber. Let not us who know that in God's house there are many mansions, but yet have no model, no design of the form of that building, wonder at his taking in of his materials, why he takes the young and leaves the old, or why the sickly overlive those that had better health. We are not bound to think that souls departed have divested all affections towards them whom they left here, but we are bound to think that for all their loves they would not be here again. Then is the will of God done in earth as it is in heaven when we neither pretermit [overlook] his actions nor resist them, neither pass them over in an inconsideration as though God had no hand in them, nor go about to take them out of his hands as though we could direct him to do them better.

As God's Scriptures are his will, so his actions are his will. Both are testaments because they testify his mind to us. It is not lawful to add a schedule [appendix] to either of his wills. As they do ill who add to his written will, the Scriptures, a schedule of apocryphal books, so do they also who to his other will, his manifested actions, add apocryphal conditions and a schedule of such limitations as these: 'if God would have stayed [delayed] thus long' or 'if God would have proceeded in this or this manner, I could have borne it.' To say that our afflictions are greater than we can bear is so near to despairing as that the same words express both, for when we consider Cain's words in that original tongue in which God spake, we cannot tell whether the words be 'My punishment is greater than can be borne' or 'My sin is greater than can be forgiven'.

But, madam, you who willingly sacrificed yourself to God in your obedience to him in your own sickness cannot be doubted to dispute with him about any part of you which he shall be pleased to require at your hands. The difference is great in the loss of an arm or a head, of a child or a husband, but to them who are incorporated into Christ, their head, there can be no beheading. Upon you, who are a member of the spouse of Christ, the Church, there can fall no widowhead, nor orphanage upon those children to whom God is father. I have not another office by your husband's death for I was your chaplain before in my daily prayers, but I shall enlarge that office with other collects [petitions] than before that God will continue to you that peace which you have ever had in him, and send you quiet and peaceable dispositions in all them with whom you shall have anything to do in your temporal estate and matters of this world. Amen.

Your Ladyship's very humble and thankful servant in Christ Jesus,
J. Donne
At my poor house at St Paul's

Letter LXXIX. *To Prince Charles*   1624

Ker reported that the Prince would be very happy to have Donne's Devotions *dedicated to him (see Letter LXXVII), and the book duly appeared prefaced by the following letter of dedication, especially important for the public acknowledgement it contains of the debt Donne felt he owed James I for encouraging him to enter the ministry. The King had, of course, encouraged him to do so, but it was a number of years before Donne had bowed to what in retrospect seems to have been the inevitable.*

Most excellent Prince,

I have had three births: one natural, when I came into the world; one supernatural, when I entered into the ministry; and now a preternatural birth in returning to life from this sickness. In my second birth your Highness's royal father vouchsafed me his hand, not only to sustain me in it, but to lead me to it. In this last birth I myself am born a father. This child of mine, this book, comes into the world from me and with me, and therefore I presume (as I did the father[1] to the father) to present the son to the son, this image of my humiliation to the lively image of his Majesty, your Highness. It might be enough that God hath seen my *Devotions*. But examples of good kings are commandments, and Hezekiah writ the meditations of his sickness after his sickness. Besides, as I have lived to see (not as a witness only, but as a partaker) the happiness of a part of your royal father's time, so shall I live (in my way) to see the happiness of the times of your Highness, too, if this child of mine, inanimated by your gracious acceptation, may so long preserve alive the memory of

Your Highness's humblest and devotedest

John Donne

Letter LXXX. *To Sir Robert Ker*   March 1625

Having been asked by Ker to mark the death of James Hamilton, a prominent Scottish courtier, by means of a specially composed poem, Donne swiftly produced 'An Hymn to the Saints, and to Marquis Hamilton'. This letter confirms what the poem itself hints: that Donne wrote with considerable reluctance, having (as he thought) given up verse for good. His claim that he would have been happier delivering a memorial sermon rings absolutely true.

Sir,

I presume you rather try what you can do in me than what I can do in verse. You know my uttermost when it was best, and even then I did best when I had least truth for my subjects. In this present case there is so much truth as it defeats all poetry. Call, therefore, this paper by what name you will, and if it be not worthy of you nor of him, we will smother it, and be

---

1 Presumably a reference to Donne's *Pseudo-Martyr*, which had been dedicated to James I (see Letter XXXVII).

it your sacrifice. If you had commanded me to have waited on his body to Scotland and preached there, I would have embraced your obligation with much alacrity. But I thank you that you would command me that which I was loath to do, for even that hath given a tincture of merit to the obedience of

Your poor friend and servant in Christ Jesus,
J.D.

Letter LXXXI. *To Sir Robert Ker*   2 April 1625

James I died on 27 March 1625 and it fell to Donne, as duty royal chaplain, to preach the first sermon before Charles I on 3 April. The nervousness understandably inspired by this delicate commission (Charles was a somewhat unknown quantity) was exacerbated by the fact that he had become used to the arrangements at Whitehall, and the new King was still in residence at St James's Palace – hence Donne's request to be allowed to avail himself of Ker's premises there.

Sir,

This morning I have received a signification from my Lord Chamberlain that his Majesty hath commanded tomorrow's sermon at St James's, and that it is in the afternoon (for into my mouth there must not enter the word 'after-dinner' because that day there enters no dinner into my mouth). Towards the time of the service, I ask your leave that I may hide myself in your out-chamber or, if business or privateness or company make that inconvenient, that you will be pleased to assign some servant of yours to show me the closet when I come to your chamber. I have no other way there but you, which I say not as though I had not assurance enough therein, but because you have too much trouble thereby, nor I have no other end there than the pulpit. You are my station [stopping-place] and that my exaltation, and in both I shall ever endeavour to keep you from being sorry for having thought well of, or being ashamed of having testified well for,

Your poor and very true servant in Christ Jesus,
J. Donne

Letter LXXXII. *To Sir Robert Ker*   3 April 1625

This note was sent in reply to Ker's offer of dinner before or after the sermon at Whitehall (see Letter LXXXI).

.

Sir,

If I should refuse the liberty which you enlarge to me of eating in your chamber, you might suspect that I reserved it for greater boldnesses and would not spend it in this. But, in good faith, I do not eat before, nor can after, till I have been at home, so much hath my this year's debility disabled me, even for receiving favours. After the sermon I will steal into my coach home, and pray that my good purpose may be well accepted and my defects graciously pardoned. Amen.

Yours entirely,
J. Donne

I will be at your chamber at one after noon.

Letter LXXXIII. *To Sir Henry Wotton*   12 July 1625

The start of this letter sent from Chelsea where Donne was staying with Sir John and Lady Danvers while the plague raged in London makes one wonder how often Donne had asked his old friend Wotton, now Provost of Eton, to intervene in cases such as the one outlined here. The tortuousness of his argument that his real motive in asking for this favour is his desire to have a reason for doing Wotton's family a favour in return, however typical of Donne, may reflect the awkwardness he feels in applying to Wotton.

Sir,

This is your *quietus est* [discharge] from me. It is your assurance that I will never trouble you more about any place in your college. But this *quietus est* must bear date from the end of the chapter, for in the letter I must make a suit of that kind to you, in which I know you will give a good interpretation of mine ingenuity that I would not forbear even the troubling of you when I had a way presented to me to do any service to your noble family, to whom I owe even my posterity. Sir, at your last election, Sir

Robert More (to whom I have the honour to be brother-in-law) had a son elected into your schools, and his place is not fallen, and so our hopes evacuated that way. Because it was my work at first, I would fain perfect it, and I am in the right way of perfecting it when I address myself to you, who have a perfect power in the business, and have multiplied demonstrations of a perfect love to me. That which was then done was done by way of gratitude by Mr Woodford, one of the then opposers, to whom I had given a church belonging to our Paul's. And for the favour which you shall be pleased to afford us herein, I offer you mother and daughters[1] – all the service that I shall be able to do to any servant of yours in any place of any of our churches. Our most blessed Saviour bless you with all graces and restore us to a confident meeting in wholesome place and direct us all by good ways to good ends. Amen.

Your very true friend and humble servant in Christ Jesus,
J. Donne

From Sir John Danvers' house at Chelsea (of which house and my Lord Carlisle's at Hanworth I make up my *Tusculan*)[2]

Letter LXXXIV. *To Sir Robert Ker*   4 January 1627

Here Donne makes a rare reference to the duties of hospitality which fell to him as Dean of St Paul's. The letter also shows a curious reversal of roles in that Donne, who frequently relied on Ker for his assistance (see the next two letters), has promised to try to secure an audience for him with the notoriously indolent George Montaigne, Bishop of London. Evidently being Dean brought with it a degree of influence of its own.

Sir,

I have obeyed the forms of our Church of Paul's so much as to have been a solemn Christmas man and tried conclusions upon [debated with] myself how I could sit out the siege of new faces every dinner, so that I have not seen the bishop in some weeks, and I know not whether he be

---

1 That is, any preferment arising in either the cathedral church itself or one of its dependent churches.
2 A reference to *Tusculanum*, Cicero's villa near Tusculum.

in case to afford that privacy which you justly desire. This day I am in my bondage of entertaining. Suppers, I presume, are inconvenient to you. But this evening I will spy upon the bishop and give you an account tomorrow morning of his disposition when, if he cannot be entire to you [give you his undivided attention] since you are gone so far downwards in your favours to me, be pleased to pursue your humiliation so far as to choose your day, and either to suffer the solitude of this place or to change it by such company as shall wait upon you, and come as a visitor and overseer of this hospital of mine and dine or sup at this miserable *chez moi*.

Your humblest and thankfullest servant,
J. Donne

Letter LXXXV. *To Sir Robert Ker*   April 1627

This letter and the one which follows it relate to the single occasion on which Donne, as Dean of St Paul's, was in trouble with the authorities. Charles I had taken exception to a sermon he had preached at court on 1 April 1627, although in this the King's hand was probably forced by William Laud, Bishop of Bath and Wells. Donne was suspected of sympathising with the anti-royalist tenor of a sermon preached by the discredited Archbishop of Canterbury, George Abbot. He was entirely innocent of this, and the matter was happily resolved at a royal audience a couple of days later.

Sir,
    A few hours after I had the honour of your letter, I had another from my Lord of Bath and Wells commanding from the King a copy of my sermon. I am in preparations of that with diligence, yet this morning I waited upon his Lordship and laid up in him this truth, that of the Bishop of Canterbury's sermon to this hour I never heard syllable, nor what way nor upon what points he went, and for mine, it was put into that very order in which I delivered it more than two months since. Freely to you I say, I would I were a little more guilty. Only mine innocency makes me afraid. I hoped for the King's approbation heretofore in many of my sermons, and I have had it. But yesterday I came very near looking for thanks, for in my life I was never, in any one piece, so studious of his service. Therefore, exceptions being taken and displeasure kindled at this, I am afraid it was rather brought thither than met there. If you know any

more fit for me (because I hold that unfit for me, to appear in my master's
sight as long as this cloud hangs and therefore this day forbear my ordinary
waitings), I beseech you to intimate it to

Your very humble and very thankful servant,

J. Donne

Letter LXXXVI. *To Sir Robert Ker*   3 April 1627

Sir,

I was this morning at your door somewhat early, and I am put into such
a distaste of my last sermon as that I dare not practise any part of it, and
therefore, though I said then[1] that we are bound to speak aloud though
we awaken men and make them froward [irritate them], yet after two or
three modest knocks at the door I went away. Yet I understood after, the
King was gone abroad, and thought you might be gone with him. I came
to give you an account of that, which this does as well.

I have now put into my Lord of Bath and Wells's hands the sermon
faithfully exscribed [written out]. I beseech you, be pleased to hearken
farther after it. I am still upon my jealousy that the King brought thither
some disaffection towards me grounded upon some other demerit of mine,
and took it not from the sermon. For as Cardinal Cusanus writ a book,
Cribratio Alchorani ['The Sifting of the Koran'], I have cribrated [sifted] and
recribrated and postcribrated the sermon, and must necessarily say the
King, who hath let fall his eye upon some of my poems, never saw of mine
a hand or an eye or an affection set down with so much study and diligence and labour of syllables as in this sermon I expressed those two points
which I take so much to conduce to his service: the imprinting of persua-
sibility and obedience in the subject, and the breaking of the bed of
whisperers [seditious people] by casting in a bone of making them suspect
and distrust one another.

I remember I heard the old King say of a good sermon that he thought
the preacher never had thought of his sermon till he spoke it, it seemed to
him negligently and extemporally spoken – and I knew that he had
weighed every syllable for half a year before, which made me conclude
that the King had before some prejudice upon him. So, the best of my

---

1 In the sermon.

hope is that some overbold allusions or expressions in the way might divert his Majesty from vouchsafing to observe the frame and purpose of the sermon. When he sees the general scope, I hope his goodness will pardon collateral escapes.

I entreated the bishop to ask his Majesty whether his displeasure extended so far as that I should forbear waiting and appearing in his presence, and I had a return that I might come. Till I had that, I would not offer to put myself under your roof. Today I come for that purpose, to say prayers, and if in any degree my health suffer it, I shall do so tomorrow. If anything fall into your observation before that (because the bishop is likely to speak to the King of it, perchance this night), if it amount to such an increase of displeasure as that it might be unfit for me to appear, I beseech you, afford me the knowledge. Otherwise, I am likely to inquire of you personally tomorrow before nine in the morning and to put into your presence then
Your very humble and very true and very honest servant to God and
the King and you,
J. Donne

I writ yesterday to my Lord Duke[2] by my Lord Carlisle, who assured me of a gracious acceptation of my putting myself in his protection.

Letter LXXXVII. *To Mrs Ann Cockayn*   May 1628

This letter confirms Izaak Walton's assertion that, as Dean of St Paul's, Donne spent each week preparing his sermon for delivery the following Sunday, taking Saturday off for the purpose of resting and visiting friends. He became friendly with Mrs Cockayn towards the end of his life, and although he was never on quite such intimate terms with female friends as with male confidants, his letters to her demonstrate that their relationship was warm and close.

My noblest sister,
    In your letter from Bath you told me so particularly how I might return an answer that I presume you intended it for a commandment that I should do so. Therefore I write, though not therefore only, for though my obedience be a good reason, yet I have another of higher value, that is, my love,

2 Buckingham.

of which love of mine to you one principal act having always been my prayers for you. At this time I knew not how to express that love that way, because, not knowing what seasons of weather are best for your use of the bath, I know not what weather to pray for. I determine my prayers therefore in those generals, that God will give you whatsoever you would have and multiply it to you when you have it.

If I might have forborne this letter till tomorrow, I could have had time enough to enlarge myself [write at length], for Saturday is my day of conversation and liberty. But I am now upon Friday evening and not got through my preparation for my Paul's service upon Sunday. If you look for news from hence, let my part (who knows but small things) be this: that Sir John Brooke is married to Sir William Bamfylde's third daughter. So, my noble sister, our most blessed Saviour bless you with his best blessings here and hereafter. Amen.

Your very true friend and brother and servant.

Letter LXXXVIII. *To Mrs Ann Cockayn*   24 August 1628

In both this and the next letter Donne is concerned to prevent the circulation of misleading rumours. His oversensitivity – as it may seem to readers – on this head was not just a product of his unusually high degree of self-consciousness: throughout his life there were people who were only too happy to believe the worst of him (see Letters VIII, XCIII and XCIV).

My noblest and lovingest sister,

Nothing returns oftener with more comfort to my memory than that you nor I ever asked anything of one another which we might not safely grant, and we can ask nothing safely that implies an offence to God or injury to any other person. I fall upon this consideration now upon this occasion. Your letter upon the two-and-twentieth of August, which I received this day, lays a commandment upon me to give you an account of my state in health. You do but ask me how I do, and if your letter had come yesterday, I could not have told you that. At my return from Kent[1] to my gate, I found Peg[2] had the pox, so I withdrew to Peckham and spent

---

1 He had been visiting Sevenoaks, one of his country parishes.
2 His daughter Margaret; see Letter LXIV.

a fortnight there, and without coming home, when I could with some justice hope that it would spread no farther amongst them (as, I humbly thank God, it hath not, nor much disfigured her that had it), I went into Bedfordshire. There, upon my third Sunday, I was seized with a fever, which grew so upon me as forced me to a resolution of seeking my physician at London.

Thither I came in a day and a little piece, and within four miles of home I was surprised with an accident in the coach, which never befell me before nor had been much in my contemplation, and therefore affected me much. It was a violent falling of the uvula, which, when Dr Fox (whom I found at London, and who had not been there in ten days before) considered well, and perceived the fever complicated with a squinancy [inflammation of the tonsils], by way of prevention of both he presently took blood, and so with ten days' starving in a close prison, that is, my bed, I am (blessed be God) returned to a convenient temper and pulse and appetite, and learn to eat, and this day met the acceptablest guest in the acceptablest manner – your letter – walking in my chamber, all which I tell you with these particularities lest my sickness might be presented by rumour worse than God hath been pleased to make it, for I humbly thank him, now I feel no present ill, nor have reason to fear worse.

If I understand your letter aright, much of your family is together. If it be so, entreat them for your sake to receive my service [compliments], which by your hand I present to them all. If they be otherwise severed, yet, in the ears of Almighty God, to whom, I know, they all daily pray, my daily prayers for them all shall also meet them all, and that's the only service which I can promise myself an ability to do to God's Church now, since this infirmity in my mouth and voice is likely to take me from any frequent exercise of my other duty of preaching. But God will either enable me or pardon me. His will be done upon us all, as his goodness hath been overflowingly poured out upon

Your poor friend and lovingest brother and servant.

Letter IXC. *To Mrs Ann Cockayn*   1628?

My noble sister,

Though my man at London might have made such a return to your man's letter from himself as might have given satisfaction enough, yet, because there were so many hours between his receipt of that letter and the return of the carrier as might admit that delay, he thought best to acquaint me with it. I am not sorry he did so, for I have found this rumour of my death to have made so deep impressions and to have been so peremptorily believed that from very remote parts I have been entreated to signify under my hand that I am yet alive. If you have believed the report and mourned for me, I pray, let that that is done already serve at the time that it shall be true. To mourn a second time were to suspect that I were fallen into the second death, from which I have abundant assurance in the application of the superabundant merits of my Saviour.

What gave the occasion of this rumour, I can make no conjecture, and yet the hour of my death and the day of my burial were related in the highest place of this kingdom. I had at that time no kind of sickness, nor was otherwise than I had been ever since my fever, and am yet – that is, too weak at this time of the year to go forth, especially to London, where the sickness is near my house, and where I must necessarily open myself to more business than my present state would bear. Yet next term, by God's grace, I will be there, at which time I have understood from my Lord Carlisle's house that the Dean of Exeter will be there, which hath made me forbear to write because I know how faintly and lamely businesses go on by letters in respect of [in comparison with] conferences. In the meantime, my prayers for your happiness shall fill all the time of

Your true friend and brother and servant.

Letter XC. *To Sir George More*   22 June 1629

Donne wrote this note as he prepared to set out for one of the two villages where he was rector (Blunham in Bedfordshire and Sevenoaks in Kent), both of which he visited each summer. Although his relations with Sir George More seem to have been generally cordial, a note of asperity, pettiness even, creeps in here, and one wonders whether at moments like this Donne found it hard to forget how More had treated him thirty years beforehand.

Sir,

The business of this church and all other business which concern me in this town determine [reach completion] this week, so that I might be at my liberty to go to do the duty to my church in the country next week but for the expectation of that £100 which you are to pay some days after that. If, therefore, it stand not with your conveniency to pay it before, because I presume you will be gone out of town before that 10th of July, I am bold to entreat you to let me know by whose hands it shall be paid me then. For besides that it were a great disappointment of my necessary service in the country to be stayed any longer in this town, so not to receive it at that day will put me to so great a trouble as to make my poor will anew and to subtract from my other children their part of this £100. Therefore, I humbly entreat you that I may hear from you before your going out of town, and rest

Your poor son-in-law and humble servant in Christ Jesus,
John Donne
At Paul's House

Letter XCI. *To Mrs Ann Cockayn*   1629?

Here Donne condoles with Mrs Cockayn on the death of her eighteen-year-old son Thomas, who had died at Bath, where he had been hidden away from his father, a fact to which Donne alludes with questionable tact in his attempt at consolation.

My noble and virtuous sister,

If I had had such an occasion as this to have written to you in the first year of our acquaintance, I had been likely to have presented you with an essay of moral comfort. Now my letter may be well excused if it amount to an homily. My profession and my willingness to stay long upon so good an office as to assist you will bear it. Our souls are truly said to be in every part of our bodies, but yet, if any part of the body be cut off, no part of the soul perishes, but is sucked into that soul that remains in that that remains of the body. When any limb or branch of a family is taken away, the virtue, the love and (for the most part) the patrimony and fortune of him that is gone remains with the family. The family would not think itself the less if any little quillet [narrow strip] of ground had been evicted from it, nor must it because a clod of earth, one person of the family, is removed. In these cases there is nothing lost. One part, the soul, enjoys a present gain, and the other, the body, expects a future. We think it good husbandry to place our children's portions so as that in so many years it may multiply to so much. Shall we not be as glad to lay their bodies there where only they can be mellowed and ripened for glorification?

The perverseness of the father put you to such a necessity of hiding your sons as that this son is scarce more out of your sight by being laid underground than he was before, and perchance you have been longer time, at some times, from meeting and seeing one another in this world than you shall be now from meeting in the glory of the resurrection. That may come sooner than you looked he should come from the Bath. A man truly liberal or truly charitable will borrow money to lend for, if I be bound to assist another with my meat or with my money, I may be as much bound to assist him with my credit, and borrow to lend. We do but borrow children of God to lend them to the world, and when I lend the world a daughter in marriage or lend the world a son in a profession, the world does not always pay me well again. My hopes are not always answered in that daughter or that son. But, of all that I lend to, the grave is my best paymaster. The grave shall restore me my child where he and I shall have but one father, and pay me my earth when that earth shall be amber, a sweet perfume in the nostrils of his and my Saviour.

Since I am well content to send one son to the Church, the other to the wars,[1] why should I be loath to send one part of either son to heaven and the other to the earth? Comfort yourself in this, my noble sister, that for those years he lived you were answerable to God for him, for yet he was so young as a mother's power might govern him, and so long he was under your charge and you accountable for him. Now, when he was growing into those years as needed a stronger hand – a father's care – and had not that, God hath cancelled your bonds, discharged you, and undertakes the office of a father himself. But, above all, comfort yourself in this, that it is the declared will of God. In sicknesses and other worldly crosses there are anxieties and perplexities. We wish one thing today in the behalf of a distressed child or friend, and another tomorrow, because God hath not yet declared his will. But when he hath done that in death, there is no room for any anxiety, for any perplexity, no, not for a wish, for we may not so much as pray for the dead.

You know David made his child's sickness his Lent, but his death his Easter. He fasted till the child's death, but then he returned to his repast because then he had a declaration of God's will. I am far from quenching in you or discharging natural affections, but I know your easy apprehen-

---

1   The younger John, not in fact ordained until after Donne's death, and George (see Letter XCII).

sions and overtenderness in this kind, and I know some persons in the world that I wish may live especially for this respect, because I know their death would over-affect you. In so noble and numerous a family as yours is, every year must necessarily present you some such occasion of sorrow in the loss of some near friend, and therefore I, in the office of a friend and a brother and priest of God, do not only look that you should take this patiently as a declaration of God's present will, but that you take it catechistically as an instruction for the future, and that God in this tells you that he will do so again in some other of your friends. For to take any one cross patiently is but to forgive God for once, but to surrender oneself entirely to God is to be ready for all that he shall be pleased to do, and that his pleasure may be either to lessen your crosses or multiply your strength shall be the prayer of

Your brother and friend and servant and chaplain,
John Donne

Letter XCII. *To George Garrard*   1 November 1630

This letter is included principally for its evidence of Donne's solicitude on the subject of his soldier son George, a constant cause of anxiety at this period owing to his having been taken hostage by the Spanish in fighting off St Kitt's, where he had been in charge of the defences. (He remained a prisoner in Cadiz until after his father's death.)

Sir,
    I know not which of us won it by the hand in the last charge of letters. If you won, you won nothing because I am nothing, or whatsoever I am, you won nothing because I was all yours before. I doubt not but I were better delivered of dangers of relapses if I were at London, but the very going would endanger me -- upon which true debility I was forced to excuse myself to my Lord Chamberlain, from whom I had a letter of command to have preached the fifth of November sermon to the King, a service which I would not have declined if I could have conceived any hope of standing it.
    I beseech you, entreat my Lord Percy in my behalf that he will be pleased to name George to my Lord Carlisle and to wonder, if not to enquire, where he is. The world is disposed to charge my Lord's honour and to

charge my natural affection with neglecting him and, God knows, I know not which way to turn towards him. Nor upon any message of mine, when I send to kiss my Lord's hands, doth my Lord make any kind mention of him. For the Diamond Lady,[1] when time serves, I pray, look to it, for I would fain be discharged of it, and for the rest, let them be but remembered how long it hath been in my hands, and then leave it to their discretion. If they incline to anything, I should choose shirt holland,[2] rather under than above four shillings. Our blessed Saviour multiply his blessings upon that noble family where you are and yourself and your son, as upon all them that are derived from

Your poor friend and servant,

J. Donne

Letter XCIII. *To George Garrard*   10 December 1630

During his final illness Donne was stung by rumours that he had been keeping away from court in order to avoid having to preach. Nothing could have been farther from the truth, and this letter to an old friend is noteworthy for its expression of Donne's desire to die while, or as a result of, preaching. And indeed, when he preached his annual Lenten sermon at court on 25 February 1631 (published posthumously as Death's Duel*), his hearers said – as much with regard to his appearance and delivery as to his message – that 'Dr Donne had preached his own funeral sermon'.*

Sir,

This advantage you and my other friends have by my frequent fevers, that I am so much the oftener at the gates of heaven, and this advantage by the solitude and close imprisonment that they reduce me to after, that I am thereby the oftener at my prayers, in which I shall never leave out your happiness, and I doubt not but amongst his many other blessings God will add to you some one for my prayers. A man would almost be content to die (if there were no other benefit in death) to hear of so much sorrow

---

1 Whoever she was, she had left a jewel with Donne as security for a sum of money; Donne was eager to be rid of the responsibility for the diamond's safe keeping.

2 Presumably as payment in kind or in lieu of interest.

and so much good testimony from good men as I (God be blessed for it) did upon the report of my death.

Yet I perceive it went not through all, for one writ unto me that some (and he said of my friends) conceived that I was not so ill as I pretended, but withdrew myself to save charges and to live at ease, discharged of preaching. It is an unfriendly and, God knows, an ill-grounded interpretation, for in these times of necessity and multitudes of poor, there is no possibility of saving to him that hath any tenderness in him,[1] and for affecting my ease, I have been always more sorry when I could not preach than any could be that they could not hear me. It hath been my desire (and God may be pleased to grant it me) that I might die in the pulpit; if not that, yet that I might take my death in the pulpit, that is, die the sooner by occasion of my former labours.

I thank you for keeping our George[2] in your memory. I hope God reserves it for so good a friend as you are to send me the first good news of him. For the Diamond Lady, you may safely deliver Roper[3] whatsoever belongs to me, and he will give you a discharge for the money. For my Lord Percy, we shall speak of it when we meet at London, which, as I do not much hope before Christmas, so I do not much fear at beginning of term, for I have entreated one of my fellows to preach to my Lord Mayor at Paul's upon Christmas Day and reserved Candlemas Day to myself for that service, about which time also will fall my Lent sermon, except my Lord Chamberlain believe me to be dead and leave me out. For as long as I live and am not speechless, I would not decline that service. I have better leisure to write than you to read, yet I will not oppress you with too much letter. God bless you and your son as

Your poor friend and humble servant in Christ Jesus,
J. Donne

1 Donne felt duty bound to support a number of charitable causes.
2 See Letter XCII.
3 One of Donne's servants at the deanery; on the Diamond Lady, see p.116 (note 1).

Letter XCIV. *To Mrs Ann Cockayn*   15 January 1631

*Although Donne writes here of his determination to preach at St Paul's at
Candlemas (2 February), he was unable to honour his engagement, possibly because
his mother, who had lived with him at the deanery of St Paul's despite her staunch
Catholicism, died towards the end of January. In the event, he returned to London
only a few days ahead of his final court sermon. Illness and the perceived approach
of death seem to have accentuated Donne's sensitivity to the accusation that he had
been neglecting St Dunstan's, the London church where he had been vicar since
1624.*

My noblest sister,

But that it is sweetened by your command, nothing could trouble me
more than to write of myself. Yet, if I would have it known, I must write
it myself, for I neither tell children nor servants my state. I have never good
temper, nor good pulse, nor good appetite, nor good sleep. Yet I have so
much leisure to recollect myself as that I can think I have been long thus
or often thus. I am not alive because I have not had enough upon me to
kill me but because it pleases God to pass me through many infirmities
before he take me, either by those particular remembrances to bring me
to particular repentances or by them to give me hope of his particular
mercies in heaven. Therefore have I been more affected with coughs in
vehemence, more with deafness, more with toothache, more with the
uvula than heretofore.

All this mellows me for heaven and so ferments me in this world as I
shall need no long concoction [maturation] in the grave, but hasten to the
resurrection. Not only to be nearer that grave but to be nearer to the service
of the Church as long as I shall be able to do any, I purpose, God willing,
to be at London within a fortnight after your receipt of this, as well because
I am under the obligation of preaching at Paul's upon Candlemas Day as
because I know nothing to the contrary but that I may be called to court
for Lent service, and my witness is in heaven that I never left out St
Dunstan's when I was able to do them that service, nor will now, though
they that know the state of that church well know that I am not so bound
as the world thinks to preach there, for I make not a shilling profit of St
Dunstan's as a churchman but as my Lord of Dorset gave me the lease of
the impropriation for a certain rent (and a higher rent than my predecessor
had it at).

This I am fain to say often because they that know it not have defamed me of a defectiveness towards that church, and even that mistaking of theirs I ever have and ever shall endeavour to rectify by as often preaching there as my condition of body will admit. All our company here is well but not at home now when I write for, lest I should not have another return to London before the day of your carrier, I write this, and rest

> Your very affectionate servant and friend and brother,
> J. Donne
> Aldborough Hatch

Letter XCV. *To Mrs Ann Cockayn*   January 1631?

The account of Donne's health with which this letter opens is not his main motive for writing: he had promised to do what he could to help Nathaniel Hazard, a young clergyman and former tutor to the Cockayn children, and this had been misconstrued by Mrs Cockayn and her sister as a promise on Donne's part to confer on Hazard the first vacant living to come into his gift. Donne does not conceal his annoyance over the misunderstanding as he explains why such an act of patronage is not possible for him.

This letter may in fact date from as early as 1625–6.

My noble, dear sister,

I am come now not only to pay a fever every half year as a rent for my life, but I am called upon before the day, and they come sooner in the year than heretofore. This fever that I had now I hoped for divers [several] days to have been but an exaltation of my damps and flashings [heightened case of low and high spirits] such as exercise me sometimes four or five days and pass away without whining or complaint. But I neglected this somewhat too long, which makes me (though after I took it into consideration, the fever itself declined quickly) much weaker than perchance otherwise I should have been. I had Dr Fox and Dr Clement with me but, I thank God, was not much trouble to them. Ordinary means set me soon upon my legs, and I have broke my close prison and walked into the garden and (but that the weather hath continued so spitefully foul) make no doubt but I might safely have done more. I eat and digest well enough, and it is no strange thing that I do not sleep well, for in my best health I am not much used to do so. At the same time little Betty[1] had a fever, too, and for her we used Dr Wright, who by occasion lies within two miles of us, and he was able to ease my sickness with his report of your good health, which he told us he had received from you. But I found it not seconded in your own letters, which I had the honour to receive by Mr Hazard. My noble sister, I am afraid that death will play with me so long as he will forget to kill me, and suffer me to live, in a languishing and useless age, a life that is rather a forgetting that I am dead than of living.

We dispute whether the dead shall pray for the living, and because my life may be short, I pray with the most earnestness for you now. By the advantage of sickness I return the oftener to that holy exercise and in it join yours with mine own soul. I would not have dignified myself or my sickness with saying so much of either but that it is in obedience to your command that I should do so, and though there lie upon me no command, yet there lies a necessity growing out of my respect and a nobler root than that my love to you to enlarge myself [explain fully] as far as I have gone already in Mr Hazard's business. My noble sister, when you carry me up to the beginning, which it pleases you to call a promise to yourself and your noble sister, I never slackened my purpose of performing that promise. But if my promise, which was that I should be ready to assist him in anything I could, were translated by you or your noble sister or him that I would give him the next living in my gift, certainly we speak not one language or understand not one another, and I had thought we had. This which he imagined to be vacant (for it is not yet, nor any way likely) is the first that fell to me since I made that promise, and, my noble sister, if a person of my place, from whom one scholar in each university sucks something and must be weaned by me, and who hath otherwise a latitude of importunate friends and very many obligations, have a living once in five or six years fall in his gift (for it is so long since I gave any) and may not make a good choice with freedom then, it is hard. Yet it is not my fortune to do so now, for now there is a living fallen (though not that), I am not left to my choice. For my Lords Carlisle and Percy have chosen for me, but truly such a man as I would have chosen, and for him they laid an obligation upon me three years since for the next that should fall. Yet Mr Hazard presses you to write for that because he to whom my promise belongs hath another before, but doth he or his Lord owe me anything for that? Yet Mr Hazard importunes me to press that chaplain of my Lord that

---

1 This is the only reference in Donne's correspondence to his youngest daughter, Elizabeth.

when he takes mine, he shall resign the other to him, which, as it is an ignorant request (for if it be resigned, it is not in his power to place it upon Mr Hazard), so it is an unjust request that I that give him fifty pounds a year should take from him forty. But amongst Mr Hazard's manifold importunities, that that I took worst was that he should write of domestic things and what I said of my son to you, and arm you with that plea, that my son was not in orders. But, my noble sister, though I am far from drawing my son immaturely into orders or putting into his hands any church with cure [oversight of a parish], yet there are many prebends [cathedral livings] and other helps in the Church which a man, without taking orders, may be capable of, and for some such I might change [exchange] a living with cure, and so begin to accommodate a son in some preparation. But Mr Hazard is too piercing [probes too deeply]. It is good counsel (and, as I remember, I gave it him) that if a man deny him anything and accompany his denial with a reason, he be not too searching whether that be the true reason or no, but rest in the denial, for many times it may be out of my power to do a man a courtesy which he desires, and yet I not tied to tell him the true reason. Therefore, out of his letter to you I continue my opinion that he meddled too far herein.

I cannot shut my letter till (whilst we are upon this consideration of reasons of denials) I tell you one answer of his, which perchance may weaken your so great assurance of his modesty. I told him that my often sicknesses had brought me to an inability of preaching, and that I was under a necessity of preaching twelve or fourteen solemn sermons every year to great auditories at Paul's and to the judges and at court, and that therefore I must think of conferring something upon such a man as may supply my place in these solemnities: 'and surely,' said I, 'I will offer them no man in those cases which shall not be at least equal to myself, and, Mr Hazard, I do not know your faculties.' He gave me this answer: 'I will not make comparisons, but I do not doubt but I should give them satisfaction in that kind.' Now, my noble sister, whereas you repeat often that you and your sister rested upon my word and my worth, and but for my word and my worth you would not have proceeded so far, I must necessarily make my protestation that my word and my worth is herein as chaste and untouched as the best maidenhead in the world. For, my noble sister, goes there no more to the giving of a scholar a church in London but that he was a young gentleman's schoolmaster? You know the ticklishness of London pulpits, and how ill it would become me to place a man in a London church that were not both a strong and a sound man, and therefore those things must come into consideration before he can have a living from me, though there was no need of reflecting upon those things when I made that general promise that I would assist his fortune in anything. You end in a phrase of indignation and displeasure rare in you towards me. Therefore, it affects me, which is that he may part from me, as I received him at first, as though I were likely to hinder him. The heat that produced that word, I know, is past and therefore, my most beloved sister, give me leave to say to you that he shall not part from me but I shall keep him still [always] in my care and make you always my judge of all omissions.

Your faithful friend and servant.

Appendix A: Glossary of Names

(THIS LIST excludes the names of persons about whom nothing of relevance to Donne's life is known.)

BARTLETT, Sir Thomas, Goodyer's landlord in London; he was a prisoner in the Tower between 1611 and 1614.

BEDFORD, Countess of, see HARRINGTON, Lucy.

BROOKE, Sir John, cousin of Christopher and Samuel Brooke's (see Letter X) and friend of Donne's from Lincoln's Inn.

BUCKINGHAM, Duke of, see VILLIERS, George.

CARLISLE, Earl of, see HAY, James.

CARLETON, Sir Dudley, diplomat; having been unwittingly caught up in the Gunpowder Plot, he cleared his name and served as ambassador to Venice and, later, the Hague; recalled in 1621, he continued to be sent on extraordinary embassies.

CARR, Sir Robert, disgraced royal favourite; he had come to England from Scotland as a page in 1603, but was quickly noticed by the King, who knighted him and then made him, in 1611, Viscount Rochester; by 1613 he was in love with Lady Frances Howard, wife of the Earl of Essex; James appointed a commission to investigate the case, which eventually found in favour of a divorce; Rochester married his mistress on 26 December 1613, and the King created them Earl and Countess of Somerset; they were later found guilty of the murder of Rochester's former secretary, Sir Thomas Overbury (a friend of Donne's), who had opposed the divorce and been imprisoned in the Tower; Donne applied for Overbury's post, and for a year or so he was in Rochester's employ.

COCKAYN, Ann, wife of Thomas Cockayn, by whom she had seven chidren and who deserted her some time after 1616; she was Donne's closest female friend in later life: his letters to her provide valuable information about his final years.

CONWAY, Sir Edward, knighted by Essex on the Cadiz expedition of 1596, on which Donne himself served; he later became a secretary of state.

DAUNTSEY, Mary, Lady Bartlett, wife of Sir Thomas Bartlett.

DANVERS, Lady, see HERBERT, Magdalen.

DEVEREUX, Robert, 2nd Earl of Essex, soldier, popular hero and patron of the arts; in 1596 and 1597 he led naval expeditions, on both of which Donne served; his relationship with the Queen was famously stormy: he served as commander in Ireland in 1599 but, beset by countless difficulties, returned home against the Queen's wishes, and from October to July 1600 was held prisoner in York House by the Lord Keeper, Sir Thomas Egerton (Donne's employer at the time); despite the Queen's reluctance to sign his death warrant, he was executed in February 1601 as a result of an unsuccessful attempt to bring down the government.

DONCASTER, Viscount, see HAY, James.

DRURY, Sir Robert, knighted by Essex while fighting under him in France at the age of sixteen; he served under Essex on the Cadiz expedition of 1596 (like Donne) and in Ireland in 1599; like Donne, he was keen to have state employment, but his quick temper made him an unsuitable candidate; he and his wife were clearly impressed by Donne's poems commemorating their daughter Elizabeth, as a result of which they became better acquainted; Donne accompanied them abroad in 1612; after their return, he and his family were allowed to occupy, rent-free, property belonging to Sir Robert in Drury Lane.

EGERTON, Sir Thomas, later Lord Ellesmere, Lord Keeper of the Great Seal of England from 1596 to his death in 1617; having heard him plead against the crown, Elizabeth is said to have remarked, 'In my troth he shall never plead against me again'; he was Donne's employer from late 1597/early 1598 until his marriage came to light in February 1602; Donne became known to the family through Egerton's son Thomas, who served with Donne on Essex's 'Islands' expedition of 1597; he was made Lord Chancellor by James on his accession.

ESSEX, Earl of, see DEVEREUX, Robert.

GARRARD, George, was, like Donne, for a while a lodger at Tincomb's in the Strand; he seems to have replaced Goodyer as his most trusted male correspondent on Goodyer's death in 1627; Donne's letters to him (like those to Mrs Cockayn) provide especially valuable information about his final few years; Donne also at some point became friendly with his sister Martha, about whom comparatively little is known.

GOODYER, Sir Henry, popular spendthrift courtier knighted by Essex while serving with him in Ireland; of about the same age as Donne, he was his closest male friend: they corresponded every week for many years; he was an amateur poet, and sometimes swapped manuscripts with Donne; on the accession of James he was made a gentleman of the privy chamber; his family owned a house and large estate at Polesworth in Warwickshire, but for many years Sir Henry was attached to the Countess of Bedford's household, and it is thought that Donne met Lady Bedford through him.

HARRINGTON, Sir John (later Lord), brother of Lucy (see below) and close friend of Donne's; he was highly popular with contemporaries; a member of Prince Henry's circle, he was devastated by his untimely death in 1612; he himself was greatly mourned when he died of smallpox in 1614 at the age of twenty-two.

HARRINGTON, Lucy, Countess of Bedford, one of the most influential women in England during James's reign, having on his accession been made lady of the Queen's bedchamber; she was a leading patron of writers: for a time Donne regarded her as his principal patron and was wary of being seen by her to be courting others; she was a minor poet herself: Donne addressed a number of verse letters to her and discussed poetry with her; in 1607 she bought Twickenham Park.

HAY, James, accompanied James I south from Scotland at his accession and was appointed a gentleman of the bedchamber, though only twenty; in 1606 he was created Baron Hay and subsequently (1618) Viscount Doncaster and (1622) Earl of Carlisle; famous for his extravagance and wastefulness, he was nevertheless extremely popular; he led a number of special embassies, most notably (in 1619) that to Germany, on which Donne served as chaplain, and which represented James's principal response to the Thirty Years' War; in a letter printed in the *Tobie Mathew Collection* he claims credit for persuading Donne to enter the Church (Donne had been introduced to him early in the reign by Francis Bacon).

HERBERT, Sir Edward, later Lord Herbert of Cherbury, elder son of Magdalen Herbert and brother of George; he was a longstanding friend of Donne's and an admirer of his verse, as well as being a minor poet himself; it says something of the warmth of their friendship that Donne wrote to him on the day of his ordination in January 1615 to share the news of the event with him.

HERBERT, Magdalen, mother of Sir Edward and George Herbert, and a close friend, benefactor and patron of Donne's; according to Walton, Donne met her when she was living in Oxford and he was still working as secretary to the Lord Keeper; their friendship was not interrupted by her second marriage, to Sir John Danvers, in February 1609; in 1625 Donne sought refuge from the plague at their house in Chelsea; on 1 July 1627 he preached her funeral sermon, an event which made a deep impact on Izaak Walton.

HOLLAND, Hugh, Catholic friend of Donne's and poet.

HUNTINGDON, Countess of, see STANLEY, Elizabeth.

INGRAM, Sir Arthur, well-known financier and a secretary to the Council of the North.

KER, Sir Robert, later Earl of Ancrum, cousin of the royal favourite, Sir Robert Carr; like Carr, he came south at the accession and was made groom of the bedchamber in Prince Henry's household; he later became a member of Prince Charles's household (he accompanied him to Madrid in 1623); he was a particularly trusted friend of Donne's (Donne gave the manuscript of *Biathanatos* into his keeping when he accompanied the Doncaster embassy to Germany in 1619).

KINGSMILL, Lady, see WHITE, Bridget.

LAUD, William, controversial churchman; he was successively Bishop of St David's (1621–6), Bath and Wells (1626–8) and London (1628–33), and Archbishop of Canterbury from 1633 until his execution in 1645; on the accession of Charles I he was effectively confirmed as unofficial chief ecclesiastical adviser to the Crown; as Bishop of London he was briefly Donne's diocesan superior, though there is no record of their relations except for the incident which provoked Letters LXXXV and LXXXVI.

LOWER, Sir William, amateur astronomer.

LUCY, Sir Thomas, longstanding friend of Donne's: most of the letters addressed to him in *Letters to Severall Persons of Honour* were in fact written to Goodyer, but Donne's son (the volume's editor) no doubt knew that many letters had passed between his father and Lucy even though they were not extant; in around 1608 he travelled abroad with Sir Edward Herbert.

MARTIN, Richard, Oxford (and perhaps inns of court) friend of Donne's; he was a member of the Donne-Goodyer circle and a wit.

MATHEW, Sir Toby, one of the more colourful members of the Donne-Goodyer circle; son of the Archbishop of York, he created a scandal by converting to Catholicism in Florence in 1606; when his father's and Archbishop Bancroft's attempts to reason with him failed, he was committed to the Fleet, where Donne and mutual friends such as Richard Martin visited him; he eventually left for the Continent in April 1608; he called on Donne in Paris in April 1612; Donne and he corresponded during the period of the Doncaster embassy in 1619; he lived in England from 1621 to 1640, when he went into voluntary exile at the English College in Ghent, where he died in 1651, having steadfastly refused to renounce his Catholicism.

MEAUTYS, Jane, waiting-woman to the Countess of Bedford.

MONTGOMERY, Countess of, see VERE, Susan.

MORE, Sir George, a man of sound Protestant credentials, he served under Leicester, travelled abroad with Sir Philip Sidney and was knighted by Elizabeth in 1597; he succeeded in 1600 to the family estates at Loseley, where he lived in great splendour; understandably, therefore, he regarded Donne – with his Catholic past and reputation as a philanderer and debtor – as a highly unsuitable husband for his daughter Ann when he found out, in February 1602, about their marriage (all of Ann's sisters married into wealthy country families); he was a member of every Parliament from 1584 until his death.

MORTON, Thomas, noted apologist for the Church of England; he was Dean of Gloucester from 1608 to 1616 and subsequently Bishop of Chester, Lichfield and Durham; Donne knew him and may have worked for him in the years preceding the publication, in 1610, of *Pseudo-Martyr* (there were certainly marked similarities in their theological outlook); Morton later told Izaak Walton that around that time he had made a serious attempt to get Donne to abandon his hopes of secular preferment and become a clergyman.

NORTHUMBERLAND, Earl of, see PERCY, Lord Henry.

PERCY, Lord Algernon, 10th Earl of Northumberland, son of the 9th earl (see below); he was Carlisle's brother-in-law.

PERCY, Lord Henry, 9th Earl of Northumberland, chosen by Donne early in 1602 to act as go-between in his attempt to placate Sir George More because of his reputation for handling such matters (he was in any case on good terms with Sir George); he was tried in 1606 for complicity in the Gunpowder Plot.

ROCHESTER, Viscount, see CARR, Robert.

ROE, Sir Thomas, member of Lady Bedford's circle; a leading diplomat at the court of James I, he was ambassador to Constantinople from 1621 to 1628.

SACKVILLE, Edward Sir, younger brother of the Earl of Dorset; he became the 4th earl in 1624; though a layman, he owned the tithes of the parish of St Dunstan's, where Donne became vicar in 1624 (Donne had to pay him rent).

SOMERSET, Earl of, see CARR, Robert.

STANLEY, Elizabeth, Countess of Huntingdon. Donne met the Countess while working as secretary to Lord Keeper Egerton (her mother was Egerton's third wife); Letter XXX suggests that Donne was unsure whether she was intelligent enough to appreciate his verse.

JOHN DONNE SELECTED LETTERS

VILLIERS, Sir George, introduced into the court in 1614 by (among others) Lady Bedford with a view to undermining Somerset's influence with the King; James instantly became infatuated with him, and was dominated by him from 1618 onwards; he was created Earl (1617), Marquis (1619) and Duke of Buckingham (1623); he played a leading role in marriage negotiations with Spain, accompanying Prince Charles on a visit to Madrid *incognito* in 1623; his unpopularity gradually increased and he was assassinated in 1628; he may have played a part in ensuring that Donne was made Dean of St Paul's.

WHITE, Bridget, Lady Kingsmill, probably met Donne through the Herberts; he continued to correspond with her after her marriage, towards the end of 1610, to her neighbour Sir Henry Kingsmill.

WHITLOCK, Edmund, member of the Donne-Goodyer circle; he visited Toby Mathew in prison.

WOTTON, Sir Henry, member of the Donne-Goodyer circle; Donne and he became friends while undergraduates at Hart Hall, Oxford; having been one of Essex's secretaries in Ireland, he was forced to lie low in Italy while the Earl was in disgrace; he was a minor poet (Donne and he exchanged their work); later noted for his diplomacy, he served three terms as ambassador to Venice beginning in 1604; from 1624 to his death in 1639 he was Provost of Eton; at the time of his death he was working on a life of Donne: Izaak Walton, who was was left to take on the task, subsequently also wrote a biography of Wotton.

Appendix B: Further Reading

For Sources of Donne's letters see Appendix C, p.130.

On Donne's letters specifically:
Bennett, Roger E., 'Donne's Letters from the Continent in 1611–12', *PQ*, XIX (1940), pp.66–78

—, 'Donne's *Letters to Severall Persons of Honour*', *PMLA*, LVI (1941), pp.120–40

Carey, John, 'John Donne's Newsless Letters', *Essays and Studies*, 34 (1981), pp.45–65

Shapiro, I.A., 'The Text of Donne's *Letters to Severall Persons*', *RES*, VII (1931), pp.291–301

Biographical and/or critical studies of Donne which make some use of his letters:
Bald, R.C., *John Donne: A Life* (1970)

Carey, John, *John Donne: Life, Mind and Art*, 2nd edition (1990)

Novarr, David, *The Disinterred Muse: Donne's Texts and Contexts* (1980)

Oliver, P.M., *Donne's Religious Writing: A Discourse of Feigned Devotion* (1997)

Simpson, Evelyn M., *A Study of the Prose Works of John Donne*, 2nd edition (1948)

Appendix C: Sources of the Letters

Burley Manuscript as printed in Evelyn M. Simpson's *Study of the Prose Works of John Donne* (details in Appendix B: Further Reading): I, II, III, IV

    Loseley Manuscript as edited by A. J. Kempe (1836): V, VI, VII, VIII, IX, X, LVI, LXXXIII

    Letters to severall persons of honour (1651): XI, XII, XIII, XIV, XVIII, XIX, XXI, XXII, XXIII, XXIV, XXV, XXVI, XXIX, XXX, XXXI, XXXII, XXXIII, XXXIV, XXXV, XXXVI, XXXVIII, XXXIX, XL, XLI, XLII, XLIII, XLIV, XLV, XLVIII, IL, L, LI, LII, LIV, LV, LVII, LIX, LXI, LXIII, LXIV, LXVI, LXVII, LXVIII, LXXII, LXXIII, LXXVII, LXXVIII, LXXXI, LXXXII, LXXXIV, LXXXV, LXXXVI, XCII, XCIII, XCIV

    Izaak Walton's *Life of Mr George Herbert* (1670): XV, XVI, XVII, XX

    A collection of letters made by Sir Tobie Mathews, Kt (1660): XXVII, XXVIII, XLVI, XLVII, LIII, LX, LXV, LXIX, LXXVI, LXXXVII, LXXXVIII, IXC, XCI, XCV

    Pseudo-martyr (1610), Epistle Dedicatory: XXXVII

    Poems by J.D. with elegies on the authors death (1633): LVIII, LXXX

    John Donne: Complete Poetry and Selected Prose, edited by John Hayward (London, 1929): LXII, LXXIV, LXXV

    Fortescue Papers (Proceedings of the Camden Society, 1871): LXX

    Cabala, mysteries of state and government (1654): LXXI

    Devotions upon emergent occasions (1624), Epistle Dedicatory: LXXIX

    Loseley Manuscript (but omitted from Kempe's transcript): XC

Index

Page references to individuals whose names, through ennoblement or marriage, altered during the period covered by these letters are here given under the name by which they are generally known or by which Donne usually refers to them; cross-references are provided where necessary.